SUCCESSFUL GARDENING

COLOR ROUND
THE YEAR

Staff for Successful Gardening (U.S.A.)
Editor: Fiona Gilsenan
Art Editor: Evelyn Bauer
Art Associate: Martha Grossman
Editorial Assistant: Joanne M. Wosahla

Contributors
Editor: Thomas Christopher
Editorial Assistant: Tracy O'Shea
Consulting Editor: Lizzie Boyd (U.K.)
Consultant: Dora Galitzki
Copy Editor: Sue Heinemann
Art Assistant: Antonio Mora

READER'S DIGEST GENERAL BOOKS
Editor in Chief: John A. Pope, Jr.
Managing Editor: Jane Polley
Executive Editor: Susan J. Wernert
Art Director: David Trooper
Group Editors: Will Bradbury, Sally French,
Norman B. Mack, Kaari Ward
Group Art Editors: Evelyn Bauer, Robert M. Grant, Joel Musler
Chief of Research: Laurel A. Gilbride
Copy Chief: Edward W. Atkinson
Picture Editor: Richard Pasqual
Head Librarian: Jo Manning

The credits and acknowledgments that appear on page 176
are hereby made a part of this copyright page.

Originally published in partwork form.
Copyright © 1990 Eaglemoss Publications Ltd.

Based on the edition copyright © 1993
The Reader's Digest Association Limited.

Library of Congress Cataloging in Publication Data

Color round the year.
    p.   cm. — (Successful gardening)
    Includes index.
    ISBN 0-89577-602-2
    1. Color in gardening.   I. Reader's Digest Association.
II. Series.
SB454.3.C64C64   1994
716—dc20   93-45391

READER'S DIGEST and the Pegasus logo are registered trademarks of
The Reader's Digest Association, Inc.

Printed in the United States of America

Front cover: Golden day lilies *(Hemerocallis)* dominate a herbaceous
border of vivid colors.

Back cover: Virginia creeper *(Parthenocissus quinquefolia)*
turns brilliant purple and crimson before leaf-fall.

Opposite: Tall pink tree mallows *(Lavatera olbia* 'Rosea') rise above blue
Agapanthus 'Headbourne Hybrids' and daisy-flowered *Felicia amelloides.*

Overleaf: The orange-yellow blooms of an evergreen barberry *(Berberis ×
stenophylla)* glow against a blue-green background of *Picea pungens* 'Glauca.'

THE READER'S DIGEST ASSOCIATION, INC.
Pleasantville, New York / Montreal

SUCCESSFUL GARDENING

COLOR ROUND
THE YEAR

CONTENTS

Year-round color Evergreen foliage provides a perfect backdrop for a palette of colors.

Color creations

Each of the four seasons has its particular motif in the garden. The crocuses and daffodils of spring give way to roses and lilies in summer; the dahlias, chrysanthemums, and asters of fall are followed by winter jasmine and snowdrops. Between these floral highlights there is an enormous range of other plants, creating a vibrant tapestry of colors. With thoughtful planning, it is possible to have a garden in which the seasons are echoed by a progression of color combinations and patterns.

Like the progress of the year, the color spectrum in the garden follows the sun. Gentle pastel shades of primroses and forget-me-nots mirror the first weak sun of spring. When the sun becomes warmer, the golden hues of crown imperials and the reds and blues of rhododendrons appear. Summer brings bursts of glorious color to the garden. As the sun gets lower in the sky and the shadows lengthen, the fierce colors of fall are seen in harvest-ripe fruit and blazing red and golden foliage. Even when the leaves have fallen, the garden is not dead; the evergreen blanket of hollies and conifers shelters blossoming winter heathers and Christmas roses. One of the most rewarding garden activities is arranging plants next to each other. Although a few plants can be isolated in their splendor, most look best when enhanced by suitable companions. Rather than scattering plants about in a kaleidoscope of colors, plan groups of complementary tones that melt into harmonious pictures. Use pastel shades to soften dramatic color schemes and to create pools of light in dark corners.

Symbols of spring Daffodils hover above primroses, fritillaries, and white ipheions.

BURSTS OF SPRING COLOR

**Rising temperatures and gentle showers bring on
a rush of flowering bulbs, shrubs, and perennials in colorful
partnerships during the spring months.**

As spring advances, more and more color brightens the garden scene until, in the warmth of late spring, it is fully decorated. Flowering shrubs and trees, woodland and border perennials, early bedding plants, fresh young foliage, and bulbs and alpines provide rich material for creating a number of colorful pictures.

Spurges, for example, are interesting plants with colorful bracts. The perennial *Euphorbia epithymoides* forms a bushy mound about 1½ ft (45 cm) in all directions, covered with bright yellow bracts. For an effective arrangement, combine it with the vertical lines of Bowles' golden grass (*Milium effusum* 'Aureum') and place yellow tulips in front.

Yellow tulips can also be paired with flame-colored wallflowers and planted in blocks at the front of a mixed border. White tulips showing through a blue sea of forget-me-nots form a beautiful contrast in the spring sunshine — or use pink tulips for harmony.

Create a different display of blue and white by setting white-flowering *Bergenia stracheyi* 'Silver Light' against a background of the airy forget-me-not-like sprays of 1½ ft (45 cm) high Siberian bugloss (*Brunnera macrophylla*). Introduce more blue with clumps of scillalike Spanish bluebell (*Endymion hispanicus*), whose glossy strap-shaped leaves contrast well with the coarser foliage of its companions.

The great white chalices of *Magnolia × soulangiana* are stained pinkish purple at their bases. This color can be enhanced by an underplanting of lungwort (*Pulmonaria saccharata*), which has pink and blue flowers backed by hairy silver-marked leaves, and the European wood anemone (*Anemone nemorosa*), whose white bowl-shaped flowers are often flushed with pink.

The blue-flowered evergreen *Ceanothus* × 'Sierra Blue,' a tender plant that thrives only from zones 8 to 11, blooms in late spring. For a pretty combination, train the soft pink *Clematis montana* 'Elizabeth' on a wall behind; in front set the white-flowered Mexican orange (*Choisya ternata*), whose sweetly scented starlike flowers pick up and enhance the shape of the clematis.

▼ **Spring bedding** Stout hyacinths, with their clear colors and sweet scents, combine perfectly with Greigii hybrid tulips, whose broad, wavy-edged leaves are striped and mottled with purple.

◀ **Spring blossoms** Pink azaleas peep through the immaculate white blossoms of a crab apple in this evocative border scene. A young *Kerria japonica* already weaves its golden flowers above a carpet of blue forget-me-nots and pink saxifrages. In fall the crab apple takes center stage again, with crops of golden-red fruit and handsome tints to its foliage.

▼ **Sea of blue** The double-flowered grape hyacinth, *Muscari armeniacum* 'Blue Spike,' steadily spreads over the ground beneath deciduous trees and shrubs. The sheet of bright blue is broken here and there with the scarlet goblets of Greigii hybrid tulips, which also naturalize well in gentle shade.

▼ **Color contrast** Cheerful golden daisies of leopard's-bane *(Doronicum plantagineum)*, carried some 2 ft (60 cm) above the hairy heart-shaped leaves, provide a bold contrast in color and form to mats of aubrietas in shades of blue, purple, red, and pink. Besides clothing rock gardens, walls, and sunny banks, aubrietas make vibrant front edgings for borders and beds.

▶ **Spring showers**
Dappled shade over rich, moist soil entices the wake-robin *(Trillium grandiflorum)* to open its three-petaled white flowers. It blooms in midspring and late spring, at the same time as its low-growing companion the trout lily *(Erythronium revolutum),* which has nodding, lilylike flowers above distinctive mottled leaves.

▼ **Majestic splendor**
The aristocrat of spring, the crown imperial *(Fritillaria imperialis)* is spectacular in full bloom. Whorls of bell-like flowers, lemon yellow in the variety 'Lutea Maxima,' are carried proudly on top of tall, leafy stems. At its feet are ground-covering *Viola labradorica* 'Purpurea' and the white, yellow-centered blooms of *Tulipa tarda.*

▲ **Harbingers of spring** The English primrose *(Primula vulgaris)* is a much-loved forerunner of spring. It colonizes in moist woodland conditions, where it is frequently seen with the starry *Anemone apennina.* The creamy yellow water-lily tulip *(Tulipa kaufmanniana)* also spreads to form clumps.

SUMMER GLORY

Blazing colors, luxuriant foliage, and heady scents epitomize the long, hazy days of summer.

After the delights of spring, with its delicate displays of bulbs and other early-flowering plants, mixed and herbaceous borders come into their own. Clumps of perennials fill their allotted spaces, and color becomes more vibrant. It is the time for roses, mock oranges, peonies, bearded irises, old-fashioned pinks, lilies, annuals, and bedding plants.

When planning combinations for summer, remember that much of the gardening year is still to come, so space must be left for later-flowering plants. Use these late bloomers' mounds of fresh green foliage, with their promise of future color, as a foil.

The choice of plants that flower in the summer months is overwhelming, making it tempting to cram as many different varieties as possible into a bed. Resist this, and aim instead for simple partnerships, using several plants of the same species for a bold effect. The result will be more arresting than a hodgepodge of varieties in different shapes and colors.

You can create a grouping by using only one flowering variety and filling the rest of the "canvas" with foliage. Try planting several corms of the hardy *Gladiolus byzantinus*, which has magenta flowers (a color that can often be difficult to place in a bed), among

▲ **Early summer** Sweet William
(Dianthus barbatus) takes over where
spring left off. Plant it in bold groups
at the front of a border and against a
backdrop of foliage from shrubs
that have finished flowering.

the low-growing variegated shrub *Euonymus fortunei* 'Silver Queen.' The gladioli will increase year after year, and their striking one-sided flower spikes will stand out against the shrub's silvery white variegation.

If you can't resist planting several flowering varieties together, here's a suggestion that will create a pretty cottage-garden effect. Combine three annuals: baby's breath *(Gypsophila elegans)*, love-in-a-mist *(Nigella damascena)*, and larkspur *(Consolida ambigua)*. Baby's breath grows to about 1½-2 ft (45-60 cm) tall and has gray-green leaves with masses of small white (sometimes pink) flowers. The blue or white love-in-a-mist is about the same height, so plant it to the side of the baby's breath. Larkspur has blue, pink, or white flowers and is best placed behind the lower-growing plants because its stately flower spikes can reach up to 3 ft (90 cm) in height. The result will be a combination of romantic pastels.

◄ **High summer** This colorful group of
low-growing plants will bloom for several
months. Dominated by a yellow potentilla
(Potentilla fruticosa) and a pink rock rose
(Helianthemum nummularium), the blue
Campanula portenschlagiana and red
cranesbill *(Geranium sanguineum)*
attempt to exceed their allotted space.

▶ **Study in pink** The perennial border phlox flowers for many summer weeks, reveling in full sun and enjoying the company of rose-pink tree mallows *(Lavatera trimestris)* and low-growing *Clarkia amoena Lindleyi.* A front edging of both matching and contrasting petunias completes the composition.

▼ **Midsummer** Backed by the tea-scented hybrid musk rose 'Buff Beauty,' this long-flowering group creates a pool of soft colors. The tall, lavender-blue bellflowers *(Campanula lactiflora)* complement the white, purple-streaked trumpets of *Lilium regale,* while their feet are shrouded in an edging of pink *Geranium endressii* and lemon-scented *Thymus* x *citriodorus.*

▲ **Shady borders** The
Himalayan poppy
(Meconopsis betonicifolia)
demands light shade
for its magnificent cups of
clearest blue. Its golden
stamens are perfectly echoed
in the shade-loving
Lonicera x tellmanniana.
Elegant hostas occupy
the foreground, displaying
their arching mounds of
golden foliage.

◀ **Sun revelers** Annual
zinnias *(Zinnia elegans)*
produce dahlialike blooms
in a richly colored tapestry,
ideal for filling gaps in a
herbaceous border. Tall
spikes of stately blue
delphiniums provide a
dramatic background
for a planting of the hardy
perennial sneezeweed
(Helenium autumnale). Its
golden-bronze flowers,
suffused with crimson, persist
through summer into fall.

15

▲ **Late summer** Strong reds are sometimes difficult to place in a herbaceous border. Here, a clump of flame-red montbretias (*Crocosmia* 'Lucifer') is successfully paired with the cerise-pink daisy flowers of the annual *Senecio elegans,* seen on a dramatic purple background of *Berberis thunbergii* 'Rosy Glow.' The airy, silvery blue leaves of *Eucalyptus gunnii* inject a surprising contrast in both color and form.

◄ **Flower bursts** After months of warm sunshine, half-hardy annuals put on a final late-summer show of color before they succumb to the first fall frost. White-eyed, purple lobelias tumble over the edges of this window box. They are good companions for the free-flowering but compact little nemesias, whose funnel-shaped flowers come in shades of cream, yellow, blue, orange, and crimson, often with spotted throats.

MELLOW FALL TINTS

**Early morning dew and fading light herald
autumn, with flowers, berries, and turning leaves
providing a wealth of color in the garden.**

With careful planning, early fall can offer plenty of interest in the garden. Late-flowering shrubs and perennials are in full splendor. At the same time, leaves are turning, fruits are ripening, and the first fall bulbs are emerging.

Herbaceous borders can be dominated by the daisy family in fall, with heleniums, sunflowers, goldenrods, rudbeckias, and New York asters in bloom. Since most of these have daisy-shaped flower heads, you should introduce contrast — perhaps the upright spikes of late-flowering red-hot pokers; the large pale pink and white saucer-shaped blooms of Japanese anemones; or the changing colors provided by a planting of *Sedum* 'Autumn Joy.'

In a shrub border, hydrangeas and hardy fuchsias are important sources of color. Other late-flowering shrubs include pretty *Caryopteris × clandonensis* and *Ceratostigma willmottianum.* Both have blue blooms, which look attractive when combined with exotic *Amaryllis belladonna,* a tender (hardy in zones 9 to 11), fall-flowering bulb with enormous pink trumpet-shaped flowers held 2-2½ ft (60-75 cm) above ground.

Heather *(Calluna vulgaris)* is another fall favorite, best grown in a mass on its own. However, varieties developed from this species offer such a wide range of flower colors (pinks, purples, reds, and whites) and foliage colors (green, gold, bronze, and silver) that you can create an eye-catching picture by using just these heathers.

For accents of hot color in the early-autumn garden, berries are hard to beat. Hips of species roses such as *Rosa moyesii, R. rubrifolia,* and *R. rugosa* are at their peak, while cotoneasters, barberries, fire thorns, and pernettyas are also coming into fruit. All look magnificent against a backdrop of yellowing leaves.

▼ **Fall berries** The European spindle tree *(Euonymus europaea)* bears a profusion of pinkish-red seed capsules that split open to reveal orange seeds. *Callicarpa japonica* offers a sunny contrast with its golden leaves, which deepen to maroon before falling.

▶ **Fiery blaze** The leaves of the fast-growing, self-clinging vine *Parthenocissus tricuspidata* turn through yellow to glowing red before falling. This plant is ideal for covering unsightly walls. In winter its bare stems are hidden by the evergreen foliage of a trained fire thorn *(Pyracantha sp.)*, which has huge bunches of red, yellow, or orange berries that persist for months.

▼ **Autumn borders** *Sedum* 'Autumn Joy' is a favorite subject for early fall color. Its pink-red flower heads and fleshy, pale green leaves are backed here by the 7 ft (2.1 m) tall, silky-flowered grass *Miscanthus sinensis* 'Silver Feather.' Vivid yellow is introduced with a clump of goldenrod *(Solidago* 'Crown of Rays'), and rich blue is added with the shrubby *Ceratostigma willmottianum.* A front edging of dark violet flower spikes *(Liriope muscari)* unites the display.

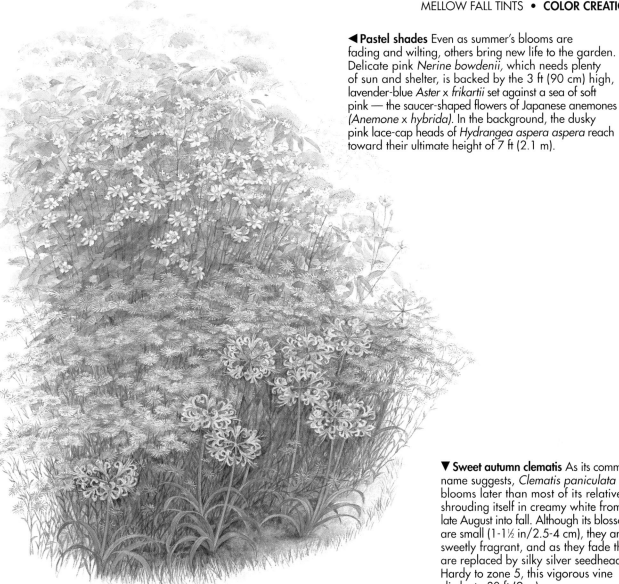

◀**Pastel shades** Even as summer's blooms are fading and wilting, others bring new life to the garden. Delicate pink *Nerine bowdenii,* which needs plenty of sun and shelter, is backed by the 3 ft (90 cm) high, lavender-blue *Aster x frikartii* set against a sea of soft pink — the saucer-shaped flowers of Japanese anemones *(Anemone x hybrida).* In the background, the dusky pink lace-cap heads of *Hydrangea aspera aspera* reach toward their ultimate height of 7 ft (2.1 m).

▼ **Sweet autumn clematis** As its common name suggests, *Clematis paniculata* blooms later than most of its relatives, shrouding itself in creamy white from late August into fall. Although its blossoms are small (1-1½ in/2.5-4 cm), they are sweetly fragrant, and as they fade they are replaced by silky silver seedheads. Hardy to zone 5, this vigorous vine climbs to 30 ft (9 m).

▲ **Pink and red** Dahlias herald the coming of autumn's morning mists and falling leaves. Available in a wide range of shapes and colors, dahlias bloom for many weeks — here pink cactus dahlias tone down the burning bronze-red color of *Helenium autumnale* 'Moerheim Beauty.'

◀ **Rose hips** Species roses, such as this *Rosa moyesii,* have a special place in the fall garden, producing large, flask-shaped orange-red hips. *Rosa moyesii* itself is a vigorous shrub reaching 12 ft (3.6 m), but there are smaller varieties, such as 'Geranium,' better suited to a small garden. Purple-pink goblets of fall crocus *(Colchicum speciosum)* make a pretty underplanting, while the canary-yellow fall leaves of the Japanese maple *(Acer palmatum* 'Sangokaku') form a perfect backdrop. In winter, when its young branches glow vivid red, this tree lives up to its common name of coral bark.

▼ **Fall cheer** Hardy cyclamens thrive in the shelter of trees. This fall-flowering *Cyclamen hederifolium* spreads a delicate pink carpet over the ground amid variegated ivy and fallen pine needles. The cylamen's own silver-marbled leaves do not appear until the blooms have completely faded.

IN THE DEPTH OF WINTER

**Braving rain, snow, frost, and thaw,
bulbs, evergreen shrubs, and flowering trees decorate
the winter garden with much-needed color.**

In many parts of the country, it is easy to believe that the garden is asleep or dead in winter. Unless, that is, you have put some thought into planning for the dullest months of the year. For instance, many shrubs stage a spectacular flowering display in winter as far north as zone 6, and the delicate blooms of deciduous trees are stunning set against evergreens that offer a variety of greens, golds, and blues when illuminated by shafts of winter sun.

Color in the winter garden gains impact from massed displays. Plant groups of miniature bulbs near the house, beneath trees, or at the front of beds and borders. The snowdrop is the first to appear, followed shortly by winter aconites: white, blue, or pink *Anemone blanda;* early crocuses; and bright blue, yellow, or purple-blue and orange dwarf irises. Plant these bulbs with tiny, pale yellow hoop petticoat narcissi *(Narcissus bulbocodium)*. Or try golden *N. cyclamineus* and echo its shape with hardy *Cyclamen coum,* whose pink, rose, or white flowers appear as early as January.

Depending on where you live, the Christmas rose *(Helleborus niger)* may bloom as early as December or, in colder regions, amid the melting snows of early spring. It's followed by the taller Lenten rose and the yellow-green flowers of *H. corsicus.*

The rock garden comes alive in late winter with tiny, pale purple-blue hepaticas that resemble wild anemones and with the white and pink flower heads of saxifrages. The dwarf primroses *(Primula × juliana)* also flower in midwinter, with the wine-red primrose blooms of the 'Wanda' hybrids competing with sturdy winter pansies. In milder regions, though flattened by rain and snow, these pansies may rise again to display their bright colors. With rigorous deadheading, these biennials can flower for several months.

No winter garden should be without sweet-scented daphnes and long-flowering heaths. In late winter, mezereon *(Daphne mezereum)* is studded with purple-red flowers, darker than the evergreen and more tender but deliciously fragrant *D. odora.* The spring heaths *(Erica carnea)* are another wintertime gem. Most

▼ **Winter sun** A harbinger of spring, the double-yellow pheasant's eye *(Adonis amurensis)* pokes its bright yellow, bowl-shaped flowers and ferny foliage through a light sprinkling of snow.

members of the heather family flourish only on acid soil, but spring heaths will tolerate moderate alkalinity. If provided with a well-drained and sunny spot, they may begin blooming as early as January in milder regions south of zone 7. Further north, gardeners will have to wait as late as May for heaths to spread their spiky carpet of pink, rosy purple, red, or white. In acid soil, heaths will blend easily with true heathers *(Calluna vulgaris).* Although they are summer bloomers, these heathers have a low spreading growth habit and needlelike evergreen foliage in shades of green, gold, red, copper, or bronze, making them outstanding ground cover in winter.

Conifers are perfect partners for winter-flowering trees, providing background color and wind protection for such delicate plants as witch hazels. *Hamamelis × intermedia* bears large flowers with crimped and twisted yellow petals. The cultivar 'Jelena' is suffused with copper and 'Ruby Glow' with bright red. The popular *H. mollis* clusters its leafless branches with golden blooms, tinged pale yellow and red in 'Pallida.' Another sweetly fragrant flower is the slightly tender wintersweet *(Chimonanthus praecox)* — hardy through zone 7. Its lime-yellow, claw-shaped flowers, appearing after Christmas, are stained deep purple.

It is the season of camellias in zones 8 and 9, where they have few rivals for the elegance of their glossy foliage and the beauty of

▲ **February color** The Lenten rose *(Helleborus orientalis)* has a mind of its own, producing red, pink, cream, or white saucer-shaped flowers, whose insides may be freckled with crimson.

◄ **Pink and white** From fall until late spring, the evergreen shrub *Viburnum tinus* is a constant delight. Pink when in the bud, the flat flower heads open pure white amid dark green foliage. They are assets prized by flower arrangers.

their blooms. In milder regions, sasanqua camellias (cultivars of *Camellia sasanqua)* begin their show in fall and carry on into midwinter. Depending on the cultivar, their flowers range from white to deep rose. Blooming somewhat later are the cultivated types of the common camellia, *C. japonica;* 'Adolphe Audusson' is among the first to unfold its flowers, which bear semidouble scarlet blooms over 5 in (12½ cm) in diameter.

The shrubby *Magnolia stellata* is slow-growing, but even young plants are smothered with star-shaped, scented white flowers in late winter or early spring, when the pale green leaf buds are still tightly curled up.

▲ **Shades of green** The quick-growing evergreen *Garrya elliptica* assumes tree-like proportions against a sunny wall. Magnificent in its full winter glory, it begins to produce lime-green flowers in late summer; by midwinter it is wreathed in a mass of drooping catkins up to 10 in (25 cm) long, which last for several months. In sheltered regions it makes an eye-catching specimen tree for an open garden.

◄ **Winter cheer** Undaunted by weather, *Erica carnea* blooms from winter into spring, spreading its neat evergreen mounds as cheerful ground cover among dwarf conifers or at the front of shrub borders. Dozens of named varieties range in color from purest white to deep purple and repay an annual clipping in late spring with even more brilliant displays the following winter.

Most rhododendrons flower during the spring months, but a few — for example, the pink-and-white 'Christmas Cheer' and the rose-red 'Praecox' — brighten the winter scene in milder regions such as the Pacific Northwest. All early-flowering shrubs need sunny or lightly shaded positions sheltered from winds. Avoid east-facing sites where the morning sun can scorch buds and flowers.

Prunus species are less spectac-ular than rhododendrons but less demanding. The earliest is *P. sub-hirtella* 'Autumnalis,' the Higan cherry, which begins flowering in late fall and bears semidouble white or pink flowers into spring.

Prunus campanulata also flow-ers early. This bell-flowered cher-ry flourishes in zones 7 to 9. Opening its blossoms as early as January, its rose-carmine blooms make it one of the handsomest ornamental cherries.

▼ **Winter colonies** The bare-stemmed pale mauve goblets of *Crocus tomasinianus* unfold at the sun's caress to reveal deeper purple interiors. Left to their own devices, in unmowed grass or beneath trees, these February-flowering crocuses naturalize steadily to form clumps.

▲ **Sunny yellow** There is no need to pamper the winter jasmine *(Jasminum nudiflorum)*, for it flowers abundantly as far north as zone 7 from winter to spring. Its lax dark green stems, however, need the support of a trellis, wall, or wire.

▼ **White as snow** The snowdrop *(Galanthus nivalis)*, poetically known as Fair Maid of February, grows wild in shady woodlands. Often taking a year or two to become established, the white bells ring out the passing of winter and announce the arrival of spring.

Leaf colors

Green is the basic color of gardening, the canvas on which all other colors are painted. In summer, when the garden overflows with brilliant colors and enticing scents, foliage offer a restful pause. Many beautiful blooms fail to reach their full impact because they are lost in front of a fussy, flowery background — foliage plants serve both as a backdrop and to complement these flowers in color, shape, or size.

Leaves need not be boring. They come in many shades, from pale lime to dark olive, from shimmering silver to rich purple. They can be as large as dinner plates or as tiny as fingernails. Some leaves are divided in lacy patterns; others grow in bolder shapes. They can be flecked, spotted, streaked, or edged with contrasting shades of green; they can also be variegated with white, yellow, gold, pink, or bronze.

While evergreen leaves maintain the same interest all year, some deciduous leaves change with the seasons — unfolding in palest green or pink and then maturing to darker shades. In fall they may take on brilliant hues of crimson, bronze, yellow, or gold.

Even during the long winter months, when in many parts of the country the garden is at its dreariest, leaves (both the usual shades of green and the more unexpected silvers, purples, and yellows) come into their own. The colors, shapes, and textures of evergreen foliage bring interest and life to barren winter gardens.

Silver and gray A somber corner is brightened with artemisias, grasses, and lavenders.

PEACEFUL GREENS

**Contrasting shades, shapes, and textures of
green leaves can create as much pleasure as a palette
of bright colors in the garden.**

All too often, gardeners concentrate on brightly colored flowers at the expense of green foliage. But green leaves are the most important element of any garden. They last longer than flowers, and they make the garden a calm, peaceful place in which to relax. It pays to think carefully about the grouping of these green-leaved plants. Choose a selection that offers contrasting shades as well as different leaf textures, shapes, and growth habits.

Green plants come in a range of hues — dark green, midgreen, gray-green, blue-green, and yellow-green — so introducing color variety is not difficult. Keep in mind that these greens have different qualities. Blue-green, for example, is a cool, receding color, which gives an arrangement depth, while yellow-green stands out, introducing welcome relief to somber shades. A variegated species, such as *Euonymus fortunei,* is particularly useful.

Try to avoid grouping plants with leaves that are similar in size and shape. Large expanses of uniformly small leaves can be boring without the interruption of bold, large-leaved plants, and a cluster of big-leaved plants appears clumsy and dull without a peppering of smaller foliage.

Varied leaf textures can add further interest to an all-green grouping. Smooth, rough, hairy, and glossy surfaces all reflect light in different ways, affecting the way in which the color of the plants is perceived.

Consider also the growth pattern of your foliage plants — the way the branches grow and how the leaves are arranged. Box, cypress, and juniper, for example, have closely packed leaves and branches that give an overall impression of a dense, solid shape. An arrangement of just these species — even if their leaves come in contrasting colors and textures — is uninspiring. But you can make the picture more pleasing if you intersperse these plants with others of a more open nature. They will allow shafts of sunlight to penetrate, creating patterns of light and shade.

To feature your leafy green grouping include at least one foliage plant that catches the eye. Sculpture plants with their dramatic leaves and form are ideal for this. In a shady or semishaded position, ornamental rhubarb *(Rheum)* never fails to stand out, partly because of its size but also because of the boldness of its leaves. If you're looking for something on a smaller scale, a good choice is *Iris foetidissima,* which has clumps of dark leaves that rise up like bristling swords.

▼ **Mixed foliage** Seasonal color and a classical look are achieved in this small and sheltered city garden with a spiky-leaved palm *(Trachycarpus fortunei)* mirrored in the pool. At the far wall, a hand-shaped, glossy-leaved *Fatsia japonica* towers above a clump of sword-shaped New Zealand flax *(Phormium tenax).*

◀ **Green and white** The gracefully arching variegated leaves of *Hosta fortunei* 'Albopicta' form the centerpiece in this green-and-white arrangement for a shady spot. They are backed by the 3 ft (90 cm) stems of the green-flowered annual love-lies-bleeding *(Amaranthus caudatus* 'Viridis') and accompanied by pure white spikes of snap-dragons *(Antirrhinum* cv.).

▼ **Green carpets** Low foliage plants, such as the heart-shaped spotted lungwort *(Pulmonaria saccharata)* and the red-tinted barrenwort *(Epimedium* x *rubrum)*, spread a luxuriant carpet over moist, cool soil. In summer the perennial grass *Hakonechloa macra* 'Alboaurea-variegata' provides a stunning contrast. In fall the leaves of barrenwort transform the carpet into a blaze of orange and yellow that persists into winter.

▲ **Focal points** The thin leaves of feather grass *(Stipa gigantea)* are elegant alone and also provide a contrast when under-planted with spotted lungwort *(Pulmonaria saccharata)*. In midsummer the grassy, 6-ft (1.8-m) plumes change from pale purple to golden yellow.

◄ **Leafy contrasts** Well developed long before the flowers appear in late summer, the rough-textured foliage of *Anemone x hybrida* contrasts effectively with the dainty fronds of the oak fern *(Gymnocarpium dryopteris)*. This anemone thrives in moist, cool conditions. The gold foliage and cream flowers of mead-owsweet *(Filipendula ulmaria* 'Aurea') add a shaft of light.

► **Green on green** This year-round display is backed by a 6 ft (1.8 m) Himalaya honeysuckle *(Leycesteria formosa)* that drapes its arching stems in summer with drooping white flowers surrounded by purple bracts. These are followed by black-purple berries and, in late fall, by purple leaves that drop to reveal bright green winter stems — the same color as the twiggy shoots of *Kerria japonica* in front. The bare stems partner a dense planting of the evergreen *Helleborus lividus corsicus,* which bears lime-green flowers from late winter. In spring the shrubs are joined by white spikes of *Bergenia* 'Silver Light' and the golden button flowers of *Kerria.*

▲ **Evergreen shelter** A background of conifers shelters the young leaves of *Acer japonicum* 'Aureum' from cold winds and the scorching sun. Maturing to soft yellow, they then turn almost crimson in fall, beautifully illuminated by the soft steel-blue foliage of a false cypress (*Chamaecyparis pisifera* 'Boulevard').

▶ **Large-scale greenery** This magnificent group has the treelike *Rhododendron calophytum* as its centerpiece. Established specimens flower in spring, with large clusters of white and purple blooms. But this plant's true glory lies in the new leaves that unfold as silvery shuttlecocks sheathed in purple-brown scales above the "umbrellas" of more mature leaves.

This foliage demands striking companions — a blue-leaved spruce (*Picea pungens* 'Glauca') behind and, at the foot, the plumed ostrich fern (*Matteuccia struthiopteris*). For total contrast in front, plant *Peltiphyllum peltatum* with its huge wheellike leaves, the graceful blue-green *Hosta sieboldiana* 'Elegans,' and *Rodgersia aesculifolia,* which has airy spikes of creamy flowers rising from rosettes of chestnutlike leaves in summer.

SILVER AND GRAY FOLIAGE

**Arrange plants with gray and silver
foliage alone or to accompany pastel pinks and blues,
forming shimmering pools of light in the garden.**

Plants with silver and gray foliage have two great assets — delicate colors and soft, velvety textures. They have a thin covering of hairs, which have developed to help the plants withstand drought and survive the hot conditions of their native lands.

Gray and silver all-foliage plants bring relief to a jungle of green leaves and offer unusual textures. You can also add a variegated species with silver markings to link the greens and silvers, binding the plantings together.

Several different silver foliage species can be extremely effective when grown together, as long as you make sure they are not too similar. Select plants for their varying leaf shapes and different growth patterns. *Eryngium giganteum,* with its thistlelike flower heads and spiky bracts, is an excellent choice. Its elegant form draws attention to any all-silver grouping.

If you can't resist adding some flower color, mix pale pinks and blues with the grays and silvers to add a touch of warmth that is not too gaudy. White, too, is a sophis-

ticated companion color — it enhances a border of silver foliage plants, creating a glistening sea of reflecting light. Good candidates for this effect are *Gypsophila paniculata,* perennial phlox, and pure-white delphiniums.

▼ **White and silver** Clumps of white flowers — daisylike *Osteospermum ecklonis (front), Leucanthemum maximum,* and the narrow spikes of *Veronicastrum virginicum* 'Album' *(back)* — highlight the gray and silver foliage plants in this herbaceous summer bed.

◄ **Shady ground cover** The dead nettle *(Lamium maculatum)* and lamb's ears *(Stachys byzantina)* together form a perfect ground cover. The dead nettle's distinctive silver markings reflect the velvety gray-white leaves of the lamb's ears, forming the illusion of light cast over shady ground. Dead nettle flowers from late spring through summer into fall, with white flowers in the cultivar 'Album' and rose in 'Shell Pink.'

◄ **Silver light** The pure-white globes of the spider flower *(Cleome hasslerana* 'Helen Campbell')* are at the center of this summer tapestry. A half-hardy annual, the spider flower is particularly suitable as an accent plant among equally tall neighbors, such as the white-tasseled *Lysimachia clethroides* and steel-blue *Eryngium giganteum*. A shimmering silver sea of wormwood *(Artemisia absinthium* cv.) provides the perfect backdrop, and the silver-gray ferny foliage of *Senecio cineraria* creates pools of light in the foreground.

▶ **Cool in summer** Slender, soft blue English irises *(Iris xiphioides)* rise above a mound of *Senecio cineraria*, whose ferny foliage will camouflage the dying iris leaves after summer flowering ends.

▶ **Foliage grouping** Plants with enchanting silver and gray foliage cluster around an evergreen cider gum tree *(Eucalyptus gunnii)*. The tree's blue-green leaves rise up over a sprawling *Senecio greyii*, whose leaves shimmer underneath. Blue is repeated in the foreground with ground-hugging hebe and in the strategic placement of a clump of spring-flowering *Allium christophii*, whose blue flower globes will turn to dusky brown seed heads by late summer.

◀ **Silver frames** The finely cut foliage of *Senecio cineraria* surrounds a pastel-colored group of everlasting annuals — *Helipterum roseum* with pink flowers and *H. manglesii* with red-and-white daisy blooms. In front tumble the sweet-scented white blossoms of old-fashioned pinks *(Dianthus)*.

▼ **Pure silver** A shrubby *Centaurea gymnocarpa* 'Colchester White' arches its silver-white, lacy leaf fronds above low-growing but wide-spreading *Tanacetum haradjani* (sometimes listed as *T. densum* 'Amani'). Its elegant feathery foliage is topped in late summer with dense clusters of fluffy yellow flowers.

GOLDEN FOLIAGE

On their own, or used to complement flower colors, golden foliage plants bring warmth and light to any garden.

Plants with golden and golden-variegated foliage look cheerful against green or gray foliage and are especially effective in shady corners. They give a warm feeling of spring and make excellent cuttings for flower arrangements. They can add a splash of yellow to places where yellow flowers don't grow well, or provide undiluted color on a much larger scale than flowers ever could.

"Golden" encompasses a wide range of hues, from pale, creamy yellow to deepest gold. Unlike the various shades of red, yellows harmonize naturally, so different shades can be planted next to one another without clashing.

Variegated golden foliage comes in many forms. It can be splashed, striped, spotted, edged, or softly suffused with spreading yellow. It combines well with green, white, gray, pink, purple, and mixtures of these colors.

Textures also vary. Golden *Elaeagnus* and holly, for example, are shiny and reflective, while the golden, mosslike *Sagina subulata* 'Aurea' is velvety and light-absorbing. With these plants, a cheerful floral effect can be created without a single flower.

Designing with yellow
Yellow behaves like white, drawing the eye with its luminosity — the darker the background, the more luminous yellow appears. It is especially powerful in the late afternoon and evening, when darker colors start to fade. Unlike white, however, yellow never appears flat or bleached out, even in strong midday sun. These properties make it a natural focal point — so use it with care. As a general rule, yellow looks better planted in single large splashes or bold groups and backgrounds than when it is scattered.

Golden foliage can be used to brighten dark corners, giving a

▼ **Sunshine yellow** As a focal point in light shade, try *Acer japonicum* 'Aureum,' which has a soft yellow leaf canopy that fans out symmetrically. In full sun such foliage may become scorched.

▲ **Rush of gold** Ornamental forms of such culinary herbs as mint and marjoram spread quickly to form dense ground covers. They need full sun to retain their golden variegations.

▼ **Bamboo screens** The vivid yellow-and-green striped foliage of the clump-forming bamboo *Arundinaria viridistriata* brings a vivid burst of sunlight to a shady spot.

▲ **Autumn yellow** *Acer palmatum* 'Sangokaku' positively glows against a dark background in fall. In winter the young branches live up to the tree's common name of coral bark maple.

feeling of lightness to spots that receive little light. Golden hops and golden-variegated ivy positively glow in the dark.

Golden foliage — particularly evergreens — can provide a longer-lasting display than yellow flowers, and this is an important attribute in winter, when flowers (of any color) and sunshine are in short supply. Golden foliage also provides contrasting form and texture in borders or beds of green foliage. It shows up especially well against a dark background, such as a yew hedge.

Golden foliage makes a decorative edging or hedge in its own right. While golden or variegated box is ideal for a low, formal clipped hedge, golden yew is the answer for a hedge on a grander scale. Low-growing plants, such as creeping Jennie *(Lysimachia nummularia* 'Aurea') or golden thyme *(Thymus × citriodorus* 'Aureus') make a pleasingly bright informal edging. Marbled hedging or edging — mixing gold and plain green plants — is a tradition, but the stronger-growing green plants must be prevented from swamping the slower-growing yellow ones.

Some golden foliage plants make eye-catching ground cover. Use golden heather *(Calluna vulgaris* 'Gold Haze' and *Erica carnea* 'Aurea'), golden lemon balm *(Melissa officinalis* 'Aurea'), golden creeping Jennie, golden grasses — or even the much-maligned, somewhat taller, yellow-splashed and spotted aucuba *(Aucuba japonica* 'Maculata'), which flourishes in the darkest corners and fills space where almost nothing else will grow.

Large-scale or bold golden foliage plants attract attention immediately. A tree in a lawn and a dwarf conifer in a rock garden are natural highlights. For summer bedding schemes, there are golden-leaved coleuses, golden feverfew *(Tancetum parthenium),* variegated busy Lizzy *(Impatiens wallerana),* and, for an impressive accent, the variegated Indian corn *(Zea mays* 'Quadricolor Perfecta'). There are also tender fuchsias with golden or gold-variegated leaves and golden-leaved zonal pelargoniums (commonly called geraniums), such as 'Mrs. Cox,' 'Happy Thoughts,' and 'Golden Oriole.' Their foliage is just as good-looking as their flowers.

▲ **Golden balm** The green-and-gold leaves of *Melissa officinalis* 'Aureum' offer decorative ground cover. Prune the plants in early summer to encourage growth of the brightest foliage.

▼ **Cascading gold** The fast-growing *Sambucus racemosa* 'Plumosa Aurea' fills a shady corner with light and grace. Rigorous pruning of all side shoots in spring results in luxuriant fresh foliage.

Tricks with gold

You can use plants with golden leaves as part of an all-foliage plan, or mix them with flowers. For an entirely gold or gold-variegated bed, choose plants with a range of form and structure, heights, leaf shapes, and sizes. Try to mix evergreen and deciduous plants to provide interest throughout the year.

Plant gold-variegated shrubs and perennials in bold masses. If they are small, the best arrangement is to set three, five, or seven plants of a single type in a clump. To avoid overwhelming the eye, separate different species of variegated plants with areas of solid-color planting.

▶ **Maroon and gold** The fast-growing evergreen *Elaeagnus* x *ebbingei* 'Gilt Edge' is a marvelous garden shrub, with leathery leaves that can tolerate wind and sea spray. It shines like a beacon in shady areas throughout the year, catching and reflecting the natural light that the somber hues of maroon foliage absorb.

▼ **Yellow creepers** The golden creeping Jennie *(Lysimachia nummularia* 'Aurea') trails its leafy stems over stony edgings. The small bright yellow evergreen leaves are a cheerful addition to taller ground covers of spotted dead nettle *(Lamium maculataum)* and gray-green lavender.

PURPLE FOLIAGE

When planted with imagination and restraint, purple foliage brings depth and contrast to otherwise plain groupings.

Purple foliage — tinted bronze, copper, or red, or so deeply colored that it approaches black — brings richness and excitement to a garden. But it is so dominant that it should be used sparingly.

There are many beautiful purple foliage plants to choose from. Use them to soften flowers with hot flame colors. Or, if the purple foliage seems too harsh, tone it down with harmonizing bright blues, violets, and soft pinks. White and yellow offer vivid contrasts — plant pale yellow with dark purples and dark yellows with light purples for the greatest impact. You can also combine purple-leaved plants with gray, yellow, or white variegated foliage.

For example, a purple carpet created by *Sedum spathulifolium*
'Purpureum' in a sunny rock garden is perfectly complemented throughout the year by the gray-leaved form *S. s.* 'Cape Blanco.' In spring, yellow crocuses provide a stunning color contrast.

In semishade, 2 ft (60 cm) high Bowles' golden grass *(Milium effusum* 'Aureum') gives height and color definition to a planting of midgreen, purple-suffused *Viola labradorica* 'Purple Leaf.'

At the front of a border in early summer, the upright, creamy yellow flower spikes of *Sisyrinchium striatum* make ideal companions for the large purple leaves of plantain *(Plantago major* 'Purpurea'). The white cups of *Campanula poscharskyana* 'Alba' provide a further light contrast to emphasize the deeper purple.

▲ **Purple and blue** Rich purple suffuses the fleshy leaves of stonecrop *(Sedum maximum* 'Atropurpureum') and extends to the fall flower heads. Purple is also the color in the flower bracts of stately *Acanthus spinosissimus;* they can be toned down with lavender-blue *Aster* x *frikartii.*

▼ **Royal purple** The deep purple leaves of *Cotinus coggygria* 'Royal Purple' are almost translucent in bright sun. At summer's end they turn glowing red before falling to the ground.

◄ **Fall splendor** The huge palmate leaves and dusky brown seed heads of the purple castor-oil plant *(Ricinus communis* 'Gibsonii') tower above the flat-topped wine-red *Sedum* 'Autumn Joy' and the slender purple-blue spikes of *Salvia farinacea.* A clump of gardener's garters *(Phalaris arundinacea* 'Picta'), with its green-and-white striped leaves, lends a touch of lightness.

► **Purple and silver** The finely divided, silky leaves of silvery white *Artemisia absinthium* 'Lambrook Silver,' a much-improved form of the common wormwood, link a purple planting of *Sedum maximum* 'Atropurpureum' with the strongly fragrant, red-and-white striped Gallica rose 'Versicolor.'

▲ **Summer exotics** Dramatic
in color, shape, and texture, the
purple-leaved garden canna
(winter hardy to zone 8) is bedded
here with annuals: rose-pink
mallows *(Lavatera trimestris)* and
lavender-purple petunias. To
keep cannas alive from year to
year in zone 7 and northward,
dig up their roots and bring them
indoors before the first frost.

◀ **Spring companions** The striking
bronze-crimson foliage of the
Japanese maple *(Acer palmatum*
'Atropurpureum') gives a dramatic
depth to the soft pink flowers of *Daphne*
x *burkwoodii* 'Somerset' in late
spring. Variegated hostas at the front
thrive in the dappled shade
and moist soil.

▲ Foliage for flower arrangers
The purple forms of the smoke tree *(Cotinus coggygria),* which has feathery, pale purple flower plumes in summer, appeal to flower arrangers. In the garden these purple leaves mix well with the white-variegated dogwood *(Cornus alba* 'Elegantissima').

▶ Bedding partners The ordinary fennel *(Foeniculum vulgare)* is a highly decorative herb, especially in the form 'Bronze,' which bears yellow blooms in late summer. The bronze foliage echoes the purple-leaved, scarlet-flowered dahlias in a design lightened with white *Lavatera trimestris* 'Mont Blanc' on one side and the soft pink of the hybrid tea rose 'Madame Butterfly' on the other.

YEAR-ROUND FOLIAGE

**Foliage is the most important element
in the garden picture, providing background and
accent points throughout the seasons.**

Evergreen trees and shrubs bring beauty to the garden year-round, clothing it in color when flowers have gone underground and deciduous trees and shrubs stand bare. Many, like camellias and the Mexican orange, have wonderful floral displays, but when these have finished, the foliage continues to supply an attractive background color. Others, such as the aucubas *(Aucuba* sp.), evergreen spindle trees *(Euonymus fortunei* and *E. japonica),* and the popular *Elaeagnus pungens,* are insignificant in terms of their flowers but valuable for their colored foliage.

Green is the basic foliage color, but it comes in subtle variations and is often marked or flushed with other colors. The amount of green pigmentation also differs depending on the time of year. It is palest as the young leaves unfold in spring. In deciduous trees and shrubs, it darkens through the summer and turns into colored tints in fall.

Deciduous foliage plants should be selected carefully with, ideally, more than temporary interest. Trees like birches and maples delight the eye with their handsome winter bark and the delicate tracery of their bare branches even when they lose their leaves.

▼ **Autumn blaze** Shortening days, warm sun, and cool nights trigger a chemical process in certain leaves that turns them from green to yellow and shades of bronze and red. The Japanese maples *(Acer palmatum)* are noted for their brilliant fall colors. The cultivar 'Osaka-zuki' is especially striking; here its fiery crimson fall dress is enhanced by the deep golden-bronze foliage of *Fothergilla major.*

▲ **Color accents** A conifer planting, displaying a diversity of shapes and colors against a background of deciduous trees, explodes in startling fall fire as the sun illuminates the brilliant red foliage. The same color is retained for months by the berries of *Cotoneaster horizontalis* at the front.

▶ **Scarlet and orange** The rapidly growing Virginia creeper *(Parthenocissus quinquefolia)* attaches itself to house walls, fences, and trees, clothing them in large, handsome five-fingered leaves. In fall the leaves turn from dark green to a vertical blaze of bronze and crimson before fluttering to the ground.

◀ **Fall symphony** Ornamental crab apples are ideal for a small garden. Some are grown for their spring blossoms or colorful fruit; others, like *Malus tschonoskii,* for their attractive shape and brilliant fall tints. Cone-shaped when mature, this crab apple looks spectacular in a shrub border, as it transforms itself in fall to a flaming torch of yellow, orange, bronze, and purple before fading away in crimson glory.

▲ **Frosted foliage** The winter garden becomes a magical fairyland when overnight frost touches the grassy clumps of red-hot pokers and ground-hugging rose of Sharon *(Hypericum calycinum)* with icy fingers. Above, the arching branches of *Berberis thunbergii* are still decorated with bright red berries.

◄ **Silver firs** Most *Abies* species are too tall for the average garden, but the Korean fir *(A. koreana)* grows slowly enough to suit a shrub border. In winter the silvery undersides of the needles glisten against the erect cones that change in color from violet-purple to brown-black as they mature.

◀ **Evergreen spring** The blue Colorado spruce *(Picea pungens* 'Glauca') raises its tiers of horizontal branches above a sprawling juniper that is busily extending its arching shoots by means of fresh green spring growth.

▼ **Gold and silver** Evergreen foliage combinations retain their interest throughout the year. With the onset of bright spring light, the variegations of such shrubs as *Euonymus fortunei* 'Emerald 'n Gold' *(left)* and 'Silver Queen' *(center)* increase in intensity.

▲ **Late spring** Warm sunshine brings out the flame-red variegations in the sword-shaped leaves of *Phormium tenax* 'Sundowner.' In sheltered gardens the evergreen clumps can reach up to 10 ft (3 m) in height. They cast a wide umbrella of dappled shade, beneath which spring primulas thrive.

▲ **Summer foliage** Purple leaves can be difficult to fit in among the strong flower colors of summer. In midsummer the almost strident deep purple hues of the deciduous shrub *Berberis thunbergii* 'Rosy Glow' need the relief of a silvery white underplanting such as *Euonymus fortunei* 'Silver Queen.'

▼ **Shrub borders** Lush green lawns circle curving borders of foliage plants accented with flowering summer perennials and edged with the brilliant tones of golden marjoram. The soft gray-green shoots of a broom contrast pleasantly with the purple-leaved deciduous *Berberis thunbergii* 'Atropurpurea.'

▲ **Color contrasts** In summer, coralbells *(Heuchera)* is topped with dainty sprays of creamy white beadlike flowers. The heart-shaped leaves, deep purple in 'Palace Purple,' are evergreen and make marvelous edges for herbaceous and shrub borders. Here their somber color contrasts effectively with the silver-spotted foliage of lungwort *(Pulmonaria saccharata).*

▲ **Silver leaves** Foliage plants are rarely distinguished by their flowers. One exception is the summer-blooming sea holly *(Eryngium maritimum),* whose steel-blue flower heads, surrounded by spiny bracts, are as striking as the finely cut silver-gray foliage. This plant contrasts well with a footing of velvety lamb's ears *(Stachys byzantina),* whose purple-blue flower spikes are of little interest and best removed.

◄ **Foliage tapestry** Contrasting leaf colors, shapes, and textures are combined here. Color variations are provided by a purple-leaved *Prunus* species, a golden-and-green *Euonymus japonica* 'Ovatus Aureus,' and a pink-tinted *Spiraea* x *bumalda* 'Goldflame.' A dwarf pine *(Pinus mugo)* and a gold-tipped false cypress introduce different leaf textures, while the graceful *Fuchsia magellanica* breaks up the solidity of the grouping.

TREES AND SHRUBS WITH OUTSTANDING LEAF COLORS

	NAME	DESCRIPTION	HEIGHT	SITE
GOLDEN AND YELLOW FOLIAGE	Acer japonicum 'Aureum'	Deciduous; slow-growing; palmate leaves	15 ft (4.5 m)	Moist soil; partial shade; shelter
	Berberis thunbergii 'Aurea'	Deciduous; slow-growing	3 ft (1 m)	Well-drained soil; sun
	Calluna vulgaris cvs.	Evergreen; summer-fall flowering	1½ ft (45 cm)	Acid soil; sun
	Catalpa bignonioides 'Aurea'	Deciduous; foxglovelike flowers, long seedpods	35 ft (10.5 m)	Any soil; sun
	Chamaecyparis obtusa 'Nana Aurea'	Dwarf, compact conifer; slow-growing	1.5 ft (45 cm)	Well-drained soil; sun
	Cornus alba 'Aurea'	Deciduous; fast-growing; red winter stems	10 ft (3 m)	Moist soil; sun; shade
	Corylus avellana 'Aurea'	Deciduous; produces winter catkins	10 ft (3 m)	Well-drained soil; sun
	Cupressus sempervirens 'Swane's Golden'	Narrow, upright conifer	15 ft (4.5 m)	Well-drained soil; sun; shelter
	Euonymus japonicus 'Aureo-marginatus'	Evergreen, dense and compact habit	4 ft (1.2 m)	Any soil; sun or shade
	Gleditsia triacanthos inermis 'Sunburst'	Deciduous; seedpods	30 ft (9 m)	Well-drained soil; sun
	Ligustrum x vicaryi	Semievergreen; summer flowering	10 ft (3 m)	Any soil; full sun
	Lonicera nitida 'Baggesen's Gold'	Evergreen; suitable for hedge	4 ft (1.2 m)	Any soil; sun
	Philadelphus coronarius 'Aureus'	Deciduous; fragrant flowers in late spring	6 ft (1.8 m)	Any soil; light shade
	Robinia pseudoacacia 'Frisia'	Deciduous; furrowed bark	40 ft (12 m)	Any soil; sun; shelter
	Sambucus racemosa 'Plumosa Aurea'	Deciduous; spreading; cream flowers	8 ft (2.4 m)	Moist soil; light shade
	Spiraea japonica 'Gold Mound'	Deciduous; pink spring flowers	3 ft (90 cm)	Any soil; light shade
	Taxus baccata 'Standishii'	Conifer, upright; slow-growing	2 ft (60 cm)	Well-drained soil; sun
	Thuja occidentalis 'Rheingold'	Dwarf conifer; slow-growing	4 ft (1.2 m)	Any soil; full sun
	Viburnum opulus 'Aureum'	Deciduous; showy flower and fruit display	8 ft (2.4 m)	Moist soil; light shade
SILVER AND GRAY/BLUE FOLIAGE	Abies concolor 'Compacta'	Dwarf, compact conifer; slow-growing	3 ft (90 cm)	Moist acid soil; sun
	Buddleia alternifolia 'Argentea'	Deciduous; arching; lilac flowers	10 ft (3 m)	Rich soil; sun
	Cedrus deodara	Evergreen; graceful pendulous habit	40 ft (12 m)	Well-drained soil; sun
	Chamaecyparis pisifera 'Boulevard'	Silver-blue densely pyramid-shaped conifer	8 ft (2.4 m)	Well-drained soil; light shade
	Elaeagnus angustifolia	Deciduous; fast-growing; silvery foliage	15 ft (4.5 m)	Any soil; full sun
	Eucalyptus gunnii	Deciduous; fast-growing	40 ft (12 m)	Moist soil; full sun
	Helichrysum petiolatum	Half-hardy; trailing stems	1½ ft (45 cm)	Well-drained soil; sun; shelter
	Hippophae rhamnoides	Good winter fruit color; spreads easily	12 ft (3.6 m)	Well-drained soil; full sun
	Juniperus virginia 'Gray Owl'	Dwarf, prostrate conifer; spreading habit	4 ft (1.2 m)	Any soil; sun
	Lavandula angustifolia	Evergreen, aromatic; summer flowering	2 ft (60 cm)	Any soil; sun
	Perovskia atriplicifolia	Deciduous; violet-blue flowers	4 ft (1.2 m)	Well-drained soil; full sun
	Picea pungens cvs.	Slow-growing conifers	30 ft (9 m)	Moist acid soil; sun
	Pyrus salicifolia 'Pendula'	Deciduous; weeping	15 ft (4.5 m)	Rich soil; sun
	Rosa rubrifolia	Maroon stems, small pink flowers, red hips	6 ft (1.8 m)	Rich soil; full sun
	Santolina chamaecyparissus	Evergreen; forms a broad mound	1½ ft (45 cm)	Any soil; full sun
	Shepherdia argentea	Deciduous; silvery scaly leaves	8 ft (2.4 m)	Well-drained high-pH soil; sun
	Teucrium fruticans	Half-hardy; lavender-blue flowers	3 ft (1 m)	Well-drained poor soil; sun; shelter

	NAME	DESCRIPTION	HEIGHT	SITE
PURPLE AND RED FOLIAGE	*Acer palmatum* cvs.	Deciduous shrubs and small trees	20 ft (6 m)	Moist soil; light shade; shelter
	Berberis thunbergii cvs.	Deciduous; compact; yellow flowers	4 ft (1.2 m)	Any soil; sun or light shade
	Betula pendula 'Purple Rain'	Deciduous; pendulous branching habit	40 ft (12 m)	Loamy soil; sun or light shade
	Cercis canadensis 'Forest Pansy'	Deciduous; pink flowers in spring	20 ft (6 m)	Any soil; sun or light shade
	Corylus maxima 'Purpurea'	Deciduous; catkins suffused with purple	10 ft (3 m)	Any soil; sun or light shade
	Cotinus coggygria 'Royal Purple'	Deciduous; purple summer flowers	10 ft (3 m)	Any soil; sun
	Fagus sylvatica 'Purpurea'	Impressive, wide-spreading tree; slow-growing	50 ft (15 m)	Moist soil; full sun
	Hydrangea quercifolia	Deciduous; summer flowering	6 ft (1.8 m)	Rich moist soil; sun or shade
	Itea virginica 'Henry's Garnet'	Deciduous; white flower spikes in summer	4 ft (1.2 m)	Moist acid soil; light shade
	Malus x purpurea	Deciduous; spring flowering; fruit	20 ft (6 m)	Well-drained soil; sun
	Nandina domestica 'Nana Purpurea'	Half-hardy evergreen; white flowers	3 ft (90 cm)	Rich soil; sun; shelter
	Osmanthus heterophyllus 'Purpureus'	Evergreen, slow-growing; tiny, fragrant flowers	6 ft (1.8 m)	Any soil; sun; shelter
	Pieris japonica cvs.	Evergreen; compact; white pendulous flowers	7 ft (2.1 m)	Moist soil; sun or light shade
	Prunus cerasifera cvs.	Deciduous; spring flowering	20 ft (6 m)	Well-drained soil; sun
	Vitis vinifera 'Purpurea'	Deciduous climber; fall tints	50 ft (15 m)	Well-drained soil; sun or light shade
	Weigela florida 'Foliis Purpureis'	Deciduous; slow-growing; pink flowers	4 ft (1.2 m)	Well-drained soil; sun
FALL COLORS	*Acer saccharum*	Slow-growing; outstanding yellow, orange, red tones	60 ft (18 m)	Moist soil; sun
	Amelanchier spp.	Early flowers; brilliant fall foliage	20 ft (6 m)	Moist soil; sun
	Ceratostigma willmottianum	Half-hardy; blue flowers, red foliage	3 ft (90 cm)	Well-drained soil; sun; shelter
	Cotoneaster horizontalis	Orange-crimson foliage and fruits	2 ft (60 cm)	Any soil; sun
	Euonymus alatus 'Compactus'	Red leaves, reddish-orange berries	6 ft (1.8 m)	Any soil; sun or light shade
	Fothergilla major	Slow-growing; rich crimson tints	8 ft (2.4 m)	Acid soil; full sun
	Ginkgo biloba	Unique foliage with clear yellow fall color	60 ft (18 m)	Any soil; sun
	Hamamelis x intermedia cvs.	Winter flowering, notable fall color	15 ft (4.5 m)	Moist soil; sun or shade
	Larix spp.	Deciduous conifers; golden/russet	to 60 ft (18 m)	Moist soil; sun
	Liquidambar styraciflua	Imposing tree; brilliant in fall	60 ft (18 m)	Moist soil; sun
	Malus tschonoskii	White flowers; scarlet fall foliage	30 ft (9 m)	Well-drained soil; sun
	Nyssa sylvatica	Brilliant fall color	50 ft (15 m)	Moist soil; sun
	Parrotia persica	Slow-growing; brilliant fall tints	30 ft (9 m)	Well-drained soil; sun or light shade
	Parthenocissus quinquefolia	Vigorous climber; scarlet fall foliage	50 ft (15 m)	Any soil; sun or light shade
	Pyracantha coccinea cvs.	Semievergreen; red, orange, yellow berries	10 ft (3 m)	Well-drained soil; sun or shade
	Rhus typhina	Suckering; superb fall colors	17 ft (5 m)	Any soil; sun
	Vaccinium corymbosum	Suckering; blue berries, red foliage tints	4 ft (1.2 m)	Moist acid soil; sun or light shade
	Viburnum plicatum tomentosum	Horizontal tiered branching; reddish-purple fall color	10 ft (3 m)	Moist soil; sun
	Vitis coignetiae	Vigorous climber; rich fall colors	50 ft (15 m)	Moist soil; sun

White and cream flowers

The art of putting plants together for maximum effect is largely a question of experimentation and personal taste. The selection of one gardener may not suit another. Still, it is rewarding to choose a favorite color and then try out other hues that harmonize or contrast with it. Monochromatic schemes can be beautiful, such as the famous White Garden created by Vita Sackville-West at Sissinghurst in England. On a smaller scale, you can create an eye-pleasing design with one or two pale-colored arrangements that introduce areas of calm and peacefulness to the garden scene.

Color is not constant, and there is no color at all without light. Because the intensity of natural light varies from season to season and throughout the day, color itself changes. White and pale cream colors are all but lost in the sharp early-morning light but come alive in late afternoon and at twilight. They are good colors to place at the far end of a small garden to make it appear larger than it is. They also enliven dark backgrounds and help separate vivid hues.

White has a luminosity that increases the intensity of surrounding hues; it mixes particularly well with the pastel shades of yellow, pink, and blue flowers and with gray and silvery foliage. It can play the dominant partner in a grouping or the supporting role that brings sparkle to otherwise dull arrangements. However, pure white can look clinical and stark next to such dark colors as purple and magenta; instead, use a blur of creamy blossoms to complement and soften such strong colors as these.

White and cream At dusk, white flowers are the last to disappear from view.

PURELY WHITE

Pure white flowers bring calm and freshness to the garden, illuminating it on overcast days and prolonging interest after dusk.

White flowers are often used to separate plants whose colors clash. Or they may be teamed with gray and silver foliage. However, there is such a variety of white-flowered plants, as well as white- or cream-variegated foliage, that you can create impressive plantings with white alone. Because whites range from grayish to creamy and may be tinted pink, blue, or green, all-white plantings are never monotonous.

White flowers have other advantages. They have a cooling effect on hot days, yet brighten the garden on dull days. They also gleam at dusk and stand out in moonlight, when other colors vanish in the darkness. It's a good plan to have a group of summer-blooming white flowers by your deck or porch, where they can be seen from indoors at twilight.

You can create an attractive scene in midspring to late spring by underplanting a silver birch tree with clumps of the bulb *Ornithogalum nutans.* At the end of 15 in (38 cm) stems, this plant has spikes of drooping white flowers that are green on the outside. Add the white form of snake's-head fritillary, *Fritillaria meleagris* 'Alba,' along with white-variegated hostas, whose foliage is particularly fresh in late spring. Choose from *Hosta undulata,* with its white or silvery markings, and *H. fortunei* 'Albomarginata,' with its white leaf edges. A group of late-blooming narcissi, such as the gently fragrant *Narcissus poeticus,* would complete this late-spring picture.

In summer the large-flowered clematis 'Mme. le Coultre' or the smaller 'Huldine' makes a beautiful backdrop for groups of white cosmos and the double *Leucanthemum maximum* 'Wirral

Supreme.' For spiky contrast, use white delphiniums at the rear and *Campanula persicifolia* 'Alba' further forward. Small edging plants might include *Viola cornuta* 'White Perfection,' scented white-flowered pinks *(Dianthus × allwoodii),* sweet alyssum, or *Campanula carpatica* 'Bressingham White.'

During late summer and early fall, when a border might begin to look tired, bring it back to life with the 4 ft (1.2 m) tall, narrow

spikes of *Veronicastrum virginicum* 'Album' and the well-formed heads of *Phlox paniculata* 'White Admiral.' Add white Japanese anemones, whose large saucer-shaped blooms can be set off with the variegated leaves of the annual *Euphorbia marginata.* Then, back these with the white-variegated foliage of *Cornus alba* 'Elegantissima,' and finish with the cream flowers of *Clematis viticella* 'Alba Luxurians' for a delightful display.

▶ **White as snow** Gracefully tall and pure white, these delphiniums create a stunning vertical element in the midst of a midsummer border. They are backed with arching sprays of bridalwreath *(Spiraea x arguta)* and a large-flowered snowy-white clematis.

▲ Peaceful corners On scorching summer days a calm splash of white provides cool relief. In the center of this design a huge clump of long-spurred columbine hybrids rises up. The columbines' golden centers are echoed in the tiny daisy flowers of erigerons at the base of the retaining wall. The foaming heads of *Centranthus ruber* 'Albus' will continue to shimmer against the dark green hedge long after its companions, the spiky white foxgloves, have finished flowering.

◄ Summer freshness Late in summer, when strong flower colors have begun to fade, this summer phlox *(Phlox paniculata)* dazzles the viewer with blooms of the purest white. The large dome-shaped flower heads persist until early fall. They provide an agreeable contrast with *Lysimachia ephemereum*, whose airy flower spikes, as much as 1ft (30 cm) tall, are held above narrow gray-green leaves.

◄ Symbols of purity The magnificent white lily is the emblem of France and is also included in religious paintings to symbolize innocence. *Lilium regale* is one of the easiest lilies to grow; in midsummer its tall stems are topped by fragrant white trumpets, which have rosy stains on the backs of the petals and prominent golden yellow stamens in the centers. Here it overshadows the flower clusters of the daisybush *(Olearia x haastii),* which continues to bloom long after the lily has faded.

▲ **Pristine carpet** The evergreen candytuft *(Iberis sempervirens)* spreads its coverings of dark green leaves far and wide. Here, in late spring and early summer, its dense clumps of white flowers are stopped in midflow by a mound of *Hosta crispula,* whose long-pointed green leaves are strikingly edged with white.

▼ **Tender white** Blooming from midsummer to fall, graceful *Gaura lindheimeri,* a 4 ft (1.2 m) tall perennial usually treated as an annual, makes an airy companion for two half-hardy annuals — cosmos, with bright green feathery foliage and large white blooms, and the white, pink-tinted spider flower *(Cleome spinosa).*

▲ **White mop heads** The Hortensia group of *Hydrangea macrophylla* has huge bursts of sterile florets in white, red, pink, or blue or combinations of these colors. Impressive as a late-summer-flowering wall shrub, its size is emphasized by a stone planter brimming with the modest but complementary *Calamintha nepeta.*

▶ **Sweet dazzlers** The shrubby but half-hardy Paris daisy *(Argyranthemum frutescens)* is particularly suitable for planters and for beds that receive full sun. Its white flowers and gray-green foliage look cheery beside the open funnels of white petunias. If regularly deadheaded, both these plants will bloom throughout summer and into fall; the Paris daisy can often be successfully overwintered indoors.

▼ **Semiwilderness** Majestic white foxgloves *(Digitalis purpurea* 'Alba') are scattered about in a partly shaded woodland glade. In early and mid- summer, 4 ft (1.2 m) tall stems hold their drooping tubular flowers in one-sided spikes. Here they add emphasis to a billowing cloud of mock orange *(Philadelphus coronarius)*, whose white blooms carry the delicious fragrance of orange blossom.

WHITE AND YELLOW

Yellows and whites make a refreshing combination, bringing a taste of sunlight to the garden, even on a cloudy day.

White flowers benefit from being placed next to a vibrant color, preferably one that catches the eye and draws attention to the arrangement. Yellow is the ideal partner because it is strong enough to contrast with white but not so different that it startles or creates a sense of disharmony.

Against the strong clear yellows of such flowers as winter jasmine, forsythia, potentilla, helianthus, and rudbeckia, white forms a striking contrast. It seems to augment the intensity of the yellow, making it cleaner, stronger, and more distinct.

Pale yellows, on the other hand, harmonize well with white, creating a gentle, restful design. This effect can be softened even more with one or two gray foliage plants, which help blend the flower colors, making them almost lose their individuality and forming a pleasing misty picture. Pastel yellows and white stand out well at dusk, reflecting every beam of the fading light, so plant them where they can be seen best.

In any combination of whites and yellows, it pays to have a few flowers that include both colors. They help link different plants, painting a more unified picture. The Japanese anemone (*Anemone × hybrida*) 'Honorine Jobert' is a plant to bear in mind here, with its white petals and conspicuous yellow stamens. Or there's the Shasta daisy (*Leucanthemum maximum*) with white petals and a central disk of yellow florets. Two bicolored annuals that are perfect for edging a border are tidy-tips (*Layia platyglossa*) and the poached-egg flower (*Limnanthes douglasii*).

▲ **White edgings** In midspring the tiny white flowers of this Bethlehem sage (*Pulmonaria saccharata*) provide an ideal edging for the yellow daisy flowers of leopard's-bane (*Doronicum plantagineum*).

▼ **Pastel shades** In this peaceful summer setting, white is represented by the tall spikes of *Veronicastrum virginicum* 'Album' and misty sprays of *Gypsophila paniculata*. Flat-headed yellow *Achillea* hybrids and, in the front, yellow-green lady's-mantle (*Alchemilla mollis*) provide soft color.

◄ **Pearly white** A perfect partnership is created by these two members of the daisy family. The large, flat, densely bunched heads of yarrow (*Achillea* 'Coronation Gold') stand like brilliant flames in a sea of simple gray leaves belonging to pearly everlasting (*Anaphalis*). Its white, yellow-tipped flowers match those of yarrow in shape and arrangement. They will grow together until fall.

► **Daisy chains** The Shasta daisy (*Leucanthemum maximum* 'Wirral Pride') makes a stunning central foil for a range of yellow and white shades. The shape of its semidouble white daisy flowers are repeated in the lower-growing sunny-flowered *Coreopsis verticillata*, whose bright green ferny foliage hides the bare 3 ft (90 cm) Shasta daisy stems. The white-and-yellow late-summer scheme is framed within a background of yellow tree lupines (*Lupinus arboreus*) and a front edging of the white flowers and white-striped leaves of the dead nettle (*Lamium maculatum* 'Album').

WHITE AND PINK

Charming pastel effects can be achieved by grouping soft pinks and reds with white or cream flowers.

Gentle whites and pale pinks create a feeling of spaciousness in a garden. During the day, their simplicity and freshness are appealing, and as the evening encroaches, they take on a luminescent quality. Although gardens with only white flowers are restful, blending them with at least one other color eases the monochromatic mood created by white.

Pinks are warmer to the eye and less clinical than pure white, complementing the inherent touch of blue that gives white flowers their crispness. As pinks become richer and more saturated with color, they appear warmer, eventually becoming dominant.

Because pinks appear darker if placed against a backdrop of white, the darker the hue, the fewer plants you should use. A large pink patch — particularly if it is actually light red rather than soft pink — destroys the calm mood of the white flowers.

When white and pink flowers are combined well, the virtues of each are highlighted. Soft pinks seem even gentler when planted with white flowers, which themselves take on a cleaner and even more luminous appearance.

▲ **Lime lovers** Dropwort *(Filipendula vulgaris* 'Flore Pleno') creates a creamy froth that rises above the bright pink flowers of *Cistus crispus.*

▼ **Summer pastels** Glowing pink *Geranium endressii* 'Wargrave Pink' stands out against the creamy white foam of goatsbeard *(Aruncus).*

▲ **Pink on pink** Two quite different pinks — the deep fuschia of *Filipendula purpurea* in the background and the salmon-pink of this astilbe — combine to highlight the slender white flower stems of *Hosta elata*. Its broad leaves contrast handsomely with the foliage of its partners.

◄ **Silver-white and pink** For late summer and fall color, Michaelmas daisies have few equals. A pure white New York aster *(Aster novi-belgii)* nestles close to a blue-flowered relation, 'Marie Ballard.' Their daisy flowers provide a foil for the graceful, clear pink blooms of a Kaffir lily *(Schizostylis coccinea)*. A silvery frame of the conifer *Chamaecyparis pisifera* 'Boulevard' behind and the foliage plant *Santolina chamaecyparissus* in front hold the composition together.

▲ Summer meadows A white-flowered cultivar of the meadow cranesbill *(Geranium pratense)* blends well with the rose-pink pincushion heads of *Centaurea dealbata.*

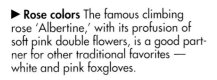

▶ Rose colors The famous climbing rose 'Albertine,' with its profusion of soft pink double flowers, is a good partner for other traditional favorites — white and pink foxgloves.

▼ Spring companions In this eye-catching arrangement, tiers of large white flower heads on *Viburnum plicatum* 'Mariesii' shade moisture-loving magenta-pink Japanese primroses *(Primula japonica).*

◄ **Summer fragrance** The damask rose 'Mme. Hardy' blossoms sumptuously in early summer with perfectly formed, scented, pure white and green-eyed flowers. At its feet, spicy pink *Geranium endressii* and the softer-hued *Dianthus* 'Inchmery,' an old-fashioned pink, pay homage.

▼ **Frothy clusters** In late spring and early summer, the clustered white heads of the deciduous shrub *Spiraea x vanhouttei* mingle closely with the graceful bleeding heart *(Dicentra spectabilis)*. The latter's slender stems are weighed down by its symmetrical ranks of heart-shaped pink bellflowers whose white inner petals protrude and glisten.

▶ **Pastel abundance** In the center of this outstanding shrub group is the floribunda rose 'Iceberg,' which blooms on and off from early summer to late fall. In late summer it is upstaged by cascades of soft rose-pink tamarisk *(Tamarix ramosissima),* a favorite in shore gardens. Its companion, Spanish broom *(Spartium junceum),* with wandlike stems of bright yellow flowers, is another oceanside favorite. The airy group is given substance with a front planting of evergreen, yellow-flowered *Bupleurum fruticosum* and a blue-flowered hebe.

▲ White and pink pillars Climbing roses — which do not climb at all but sprawl unless tied to supports — include a group known as pillar roses. They have stiff but supple shoots that are less vigorous than other large-flowered climbers. When they are wound around and tied to upright supports, they look spectacular, becoming dramatic living columns covered from top to bottom in clusters of blooms.

▶ Autumn walkway The Japanese anemones (*Anemone x hybrida*) fill a fall border with charm. Modern hybrids spread to form neat clumps of vinelike dark green foliage, above which rise weaving wands of saucer-shaped blooms with golden yellow stamens. The pure white 'Honorine Jobert' is an old favorite, mingling with the cool pink of 'Queen Charlotte.'

WHITE AND BLUE

White flowers give depth to all shades of blue, throwing the dusky blues into sharp relief.

Blue flowers bring to mind sunlit skies and the early days of the growing season, when the garden starts coming to life. White gives blue a greater clarity, whether it is the pale blue of *Mertensia virginica* or the intense blue of *Gentiana verna*. The freshness of blue flowers planted with white in woodland is one of the delights of spring. For example, masses of white and clear deep blue *Anemone apennina* illuminated by the dappled light beneath deciduous trees are a stunning sight.

One of the best pairings for a spring bed is a carpet of forget-me-nots pierced with white tulips. This simple composition provides an intriguing contrast between the plain forget-me-nots and the tulips' large, elegant goblets.

In early summer, statuesque spikes of blue delphiniums behind double white peonies and the luminous flowers of *Geranium* 'Johnson's Blue' again provide a contrast in flower form. The violet-blue *Geranium* × *magnificum* is another hardy cranesbill, with mounded form and lobed leaves that combine well with the narrow, upright foliage of white *Iris sibirica*.

Blue flowers are less common once summer ends, but there are still some choices. In early fall, 3 ft (1 m) high monkshood (*Aconitum* 'Bressingham Spire'), with violet-blue hooded flowers, contrasts well with two equally imposing plants: the white bottle-brush flowers of bugbane (*Cimicifuga racemosa*) and giant white late-blooming daisies of *Chrysanthemum serotinum*.

▲ **Late-summer partners**
The silky blooms of musk mallow *(Malva moschata* 'Alba'*)* glow white behind clouds of purplish-blue sea lavender *(Limonium latifolium)*. Easy and undemanding to grow, the flower sprays can be preserved in dried arrangements.

▼ **Woodland spring** Thriving in the moist soil and dappled shade of deciduous trees, these woodland plants make charming companions. The white three-petaled blooms of wake-robin *(Trillium grandiflorum)* contrast in form and color with the nodding bluebells *(Endymion non-scriptus)*.

▶ **Close friends** Sweet alyssum *(Lobularia maritima)* is a popular edging plant with its dense, fragrant, and long-lasting white flowers. It is frequently paired with another annual, lobelia, which comes in a range of blue shades — dark blue 'Crystal Palace,' midblue 'Blue Stone,' and pale 'Cambridge Blue.'

▼ **Winter in the rock garden** Spring comes early with little nodding snowflakes *(Leucojum vernum)* nestling close to the blue anemone lookalike, *Hepatica nobilis.* Both need moist soil and shade.

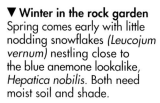

▶ **Waterfront beauties** Lush clumps of grassy foliage tumble over the water's edge. In the shimmering sunlight reflected in this pond's smooth surface, weaving water irises *(Iris laevigata* 'Alba') show off their magnificent blue-purple and white blooms.

▼ **White abandon** The fragrant rambler rose 'Sander's White' scrambles in a sea of shining lavender flax *(Linum narbonense),* which is studded at intervals with the huge, dark purple flower heads of *Allium christophii.* On the right, the spiny foliage of bear's-breeches *(Acanthus spinosissimus)* gives strength to the grouping.

▶ **Pearly white** In late spring the arching branches of
the alkaline-hating deciduous shrub *Exochorda racemosa*
are laden with dense clusters of pure white blooms. Each
flower is up to 1½ in (4 cm) across and opens from globular
buds that give the shrub its common name of pearl bush.
Its branches reach down to touch the deep purplish-blue
tubular flowers of Bethlehem sage *(Pulmonaria saccharata)*,
which has silver-marked lance-shaped leaves.

◀ **Year-round pleasure** The evergreen willowleaf
cotoneaster *(Cotoneaster salicifolius)* arches its branches
to create a pool of shade. In late spring the white bell-
shaped flowers of Solomon's seal *(Polygonatum)* hang
beneath pale green ribbed leaves. They are followed
by batches of blue bellflowers *(Campanula persicifolia)*,
flowering with the cotoneaster's billowing white clouds.
Much later, clusters of scarlet berries take over.
If the birds permit, the fruit lasts well into the winter.

WHITE THROUGH THE YEAR

White blooms every month, brightening winter-dreary gardens and providing serene contrasts for summer profusion.

In the winter and spring garden white flowers predominate, taking on a translucence that is lacking in the ice-cool whites of summer. Few sights are more welcome than the first snowdrops *(Galanthus nivalis)*. They are a sure sign that spring is on the way, and they are soon joined by pale cream primroses, crocuses, hyacinths, narcissi, and tulips. Later come the white scented stars of *Magnolia stellata* and the hazy clouds of *Amelanchier canadensis*.

As the sun gets warmer and the light stronger, white flowers become ever crisper and their scent heavier until the end of spring, when the garden is perfumed with top-heavy white lilacs, dainty lilies of the valley, and the massed flowers of the mock orange *(Philadelphus)*. The ornamental thorn *(Crataegus monogyna)* is smothered with white blossoms that have such a strong and pungent scent they are nearly overpowering.

As summer continues, there is much to anticipate: the pure white open bells of the shrubby *Deutzia × lemoinei*, roses, lilies, and snow-in-summer *(Cerastium tomentosum)*, which threatens to overrun its allotted space. Late summer sees the creamy white clusters on evergreen *Eucryphia × nymansensis,* the spikes of the butterfly bush *(Buddleia davidii* 'White Cloud'), and the California tree poppy *(Romneya coulteri)*, whose petals resemble crushed silk.

In fall the white tones become soft again — creamy in the silky plumes of pampas grass *(Cortaderia selloana)* and the scented evergreen *Osmanthus heterophyllus;* soft white in the little fall crocus *(Colchicum speciosum* 'Album'). The winter scene is brightened considerably with white-flowering evergreens like ericas, *Viburnum × burkwoodii,* and the fragrant *Daphne odora* 'Alba.'

▼ **Summer's end** Tall lace-cap hydrangeas thrive in coastal gardens, displaying their flat flower heads above dark green foliage for several months before fading to russet shades.

▶ **Fall mists** A cloud of the tiny, double white flowers of perennial baby's breath (*Gypsophila paniculata* 'Bristol Fairy') creates a misty background for the bronze-red daisylike flowers of *Helenium autumnale* 'Moerheim Beauty.' Both are long lasting as cut flowers.

▲ **Shades of autumn** The creamy feathery plumes of pampas grass (*Cortaderia selloana*) steal the scene in this impressive fall planting. But on the left, the variegated foliage of a bold clump of zebra grass (*Miscanthus sinensis* 'Zebrinus') adds a spicy touch. In front, the slender stems of the half-hardy fountain grass (*Pennisetum setaceum*), set with slender, silky cream spikes, add another dimension to an all-grass theme.

◀ **Winter joy** The common snowdrop, as its name suggests, is one of the earliest-blooming bulbs. Plant it in sandy, rich soil in full sun or underneath deciduous trees. When transferred from one spot to another, it takes its time to settle down again. But once it is established, it will push its familiar white bells above ground during late winter and spread to form cheery carpets of flowers.

▲ **Frosty white** The flowering Fuji cherry, *Prunus incisa*, blooms in late winter, studding its naked branches with pale pink buds that open into pure white flowers. The small, toothed leaves are spectacularly colored in fall. This Japanese plant is often cultivated as a bonsai specimen.

◄ **Christmas blooms** Set in a sheltered location — for example, up against a house foundation — the Christmas rose *(Helleborus niger)* may indeed open its roselike flowers in December, even in New England. Set amid handsome evergreen foliage, this perennial's shiny, satiny petals — often stained rose-purple at the base — arrange themselves around a center of golden anthers.

▲ **Spring harbingers** The pure white and clear blue flowers of the little *Anemone apennina* held on slender stems above ferny foliage, dominate a spring border carpeted with lilac *Scilla siberica*. These pastel shades soften the rich maroon cups of the Lenten rose *(Helleborus orientalis)*.

▶ **April showers** The spectacular blossoms of a flowering cherry tree will soon cast their white petals over a planting of cream and golden narcissi trumpets mingled with the full blooms of red and yellow cottage tulips. These flowers are the epitome of a traditional spring garden.

▲ **May blossoms** The sweetly scented garden lilacs are cultivars of *Syringa vulgaris* that have been specially bred for their pure colors. These can range from white, cream, and yellow through all the shades of pink, red, blue, and purple. Here, dense, pure white panicles contrast effectively in form and color with a neighboring rose-pink rhododendron.

◄ **Summer snow** In spite of its name, the summer snowflake *(Leucojum aestivum)*, with its sprays of nodding bell-like flowers, blooms in April and May, at the same time as the striking orange tulip 'General de Wet.' The snowflake's narrow dark green leaves contrast well with the broader, lighter green tulip foliage.

▲ **Spring skies** The pure white flowers of the fragrant *Daphne mezereum* 'Alba' rising above the intense blue bells of *Scilla siberica* 'Spring Beauty' suggest images of clouds in a blue March sky.

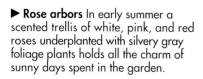

▶ **Rose arbors** In early summer a scented trellis of white, pink, and red roses underplanted with silvery gray foliage plants holds all the charm of sunny days spent in the garden.

▼ **Summer perfection** In this early summer scene, an edging of nicotianas is balanced by an urn of marguerites *(Argyranthemum frutescens)*, while a backdrop of *Viburnum x carlcephalum* suggests the majesty of rhododendrons.

WHITE AND CREAM FLOWERS

	NAME	DESCRIPTION AND SITE	HEIGHT	SEASON
TREES	Arbutus unedo	Evergreen glossy foliage; loamy soil; sun	15 ft (4.5 m)	Fall
	Catalpa bignonioides	Deciduous; long seedpods; any soil; sun	40 ft (12 m)	Summer
	Halesia carolina, H. monticola	Deciduous; moist acid soil; sun	40 ft (12 m)	Spring
	Malus hupehensis, M. x robusta	Deciduous; fall fruit; any soil; sun	20-40 ft (6-12 m)	Spring
	Sophora japonica 'Regent'	Deciduous; loamy soil; sun; shelter	50 ft (15 m)	Late summer
	Sorbus spp. and cvs.	Deciduous; fall tints/berries; any soil; sun	40 ft (12 m)	Spring
	Stewartia spp.	Deciduous; fall tints, interesting bark; acid soil	12-20 ft (3.6-6 m)	Summer
	Styrax japonicus	Deciduous; moist acid soil; sun; shelter	25 ft (7.5 m)	Late spring
SHRUBS	Abelia x grandiflora	Semievergreen; moist acid soil; sun; shelter	3-6 ft (90-180 cm)	Summer–fall
	Carpenteria californica	Evergreen; loamy soil; full sun	6 ft (1.8 m)	Summer
	Choisya ternata	Evergreen; loamy soil; sun; shelter	7 ft (2.1 m)	Late spring
	Clematis spp. and cvs.	Hardy deciduous climbers; neutral soil; sun	6-20 ft (1.8-6 m)	Spring–fall
	Clethra alnifolia	Deciduous; rich, moist acid soil; sun or shade	4-8 ft (1.2-2.4 m)	Summer
	Cornus florida	Deciduous; moist acid soil; sun or light shade	10-25 ft (3-7.5 m)	Late spring
	Corynabutilon vitifolium 'Album'	Evergreen; any soil; sunny wall	10-25 ft (3-7.5 m)	Spring–fall
	Cytisus x kewensis	Deciduous, spreading; well-drained soil; full sun	1-2 ft (30-60 cm)	Spring
	Deutzia gracilis	Deciduous; any soil; sun or light shade	2-4 ft (60-120 cm)	Late spring
	Helianthemum nummularium cvs.	Evergreen; well-drained soil; full sun	1-2 ft (30-60 cm)	Late spring
	Hoheria glabrata	Deciduous; half-hardy; any soil; sun; shelter	30 ft (9 m)	Summer
	Hydrangea arborescens 'Grandiflora'	Deciduous; moist, well-drained loam; sun or light shade	4-6 ft (1.2-1.8 m)	Summer–fall
	Jasminum officinale	Deciduous climber; well-drained soil; shelter	15-30 ft (4.5-9 m)	Summer–fall
	Leucothoe fontanesiana	Evergreen; moist, well-drained acid soil; shade	4 ft (1.2 m)	Late spring
	Lonicera fragrantissima	Semievergreen, scented; well-drained soil; sun	6-10 ft (1.8-3 m)	Late winter–spring
	Magnolia spp. and cvs.	Deciduous; well-drained loam; shelter	6-50 ft (1.8-15 m)	Spring–summer
	Osmanthus x fortunei	Evergreen; well-drained acid soil; sun; shelter	15-20 ft (4.5-6 m)	Fall
	Pieris spp. and cvs.	Evergreen, young leaves red; acid soil; shelter	8-12 ft (2.4-3.6 m)	Spring
	Polygonum aubertii	Deciduous strong climber; any soil; sun or shade	30 ft (9 m)	Summer–fall
	Prunus spp., numerous cvs.	Deciduous; good fall tints, bark; moist, well-drained soil; sun	4-20 ft (1.2-6 m)	Spring
	Rhodotypos scandens	Deciduous; any soil; sun or light shade	3-6 ft (90-180 cm)	Late spring
	Ribes sanguineum 'Album'	Deciduous; moist, well-drained soil; sun	6-10 ft (1.8-3 m)	Spring
	Rubus parviflorus	Deciduous, fast-growing; any soil; sun	6-7 ft (1.8-2.1 m)	Late spring–summer
	Skimmia japonica, S. reevesiana	Evergreen, berries; rich, moist acid soil; partial shade	1½-5 ft (45-150 cm)	Spring
	Sorbaria aitchisonii	Deciduous, ferny leaves; moist, well-drained soil; sun or shade	6-9 ft (1.8-2.7 m)	Summer
	Trachelospermum jasminoides	Evergreen climber; fragrant; acid soil; warm wall	10-12 ft (3-3.6 m)	Summer
	Vinca minor 'Alba'	Evergreen ground cover; any soil; shade	2-4 in (5-10 cm)	Spring–fall
	Weigela 'Bristol Snowflake'	Deciduous; well-drained soil; sun	6-9 ft (1.8-2.7 m)	Early summer
	Wisteria sinensis alba	Deciduous climber; deep soil; sunny wall	25 ft (7.5 m)	Spring–summer

NAME	DESCRIPTION AND SITE	HEIGHT	SEASON
Achillea ptarmica 'The Pearl'	Wide-spreading; well-drained soil; sun	2½ ft (75 cm)	Late summer
Anaphalis spp.	Silvery leaves; well-drained soil; sun	1-2 ft (30-60 cm)	Summer–fall
Androsace carnea	Evergreen rock plant; well-drained soil; sun	1-4 in (2.5-10 cm)	Early summer
Anthemis cupaniana	Gray foliage; slightly alkaline soil; sun	1 ft (30 cm)	All summer
Arabis caucasica	Evergreen rock plant; well-drained soil; shade	4-9 in (10-23 cm)	Late winter–spring
Arenaria balearica, A. montana	Evergreen rock plants; gritty soil; shade	1-6 in (2.5-15 cm)	Spring–summer
Aruncus dioicus	Dramatic feathery flowers; moist soil; shade	4-6 ft (1.2-1.8 m)	Summer
Astilbe spp. and cvs.	Handsome foliage; moist soil; sun or light shade	1½-4 ft (45-120 cm)	Summer
Camassia leichtlinii 'Plena'	Bulbous; rich, moist soil; sun or light shade	3 ft (90 cm)	Summer
Cerastium tomentosum	Silvery white carpet; well-drained soil; sun	6-8 in (15-20 cm)	Early summer
Cimicifuga spp.	Handsome foliage; rich, moist soil; light shade	2-6 ft (60-180 cm)	Summer–fall
Clematis recta	Border plant, scented; ordinary soil; sun	4 ft (1.2 m)	Summer
Convallaria majalis	Fragrant lily of the valley; moist soil; shade	6-8 in (15-20 cm)	Late spring
Crambe cordifolia	Huge heart-shaped leaves; rich, well-drained soil; sun	6 ft (1.8 m)	Early summer
Dictamnus albus	Lemon-scented; volatile oils; loamy soil; sun	2-3 ft (60-90 cm)	Summer
Dryas octopetala	Evergreen rock plant; well-drained soil; sun	3-8 in (7.5-20 cm)	Summer
Filipendula ulmaria	Large palmate leaves; moist soil; sun or light shade	3 ft (90 cm)	Summer
Galium odoratum	Ground-cover plant; moist soil; sun or shade	10 in (25 cm)	Spring–summer
Galtonia candicans	Bulbous; rich soil; full sun	4 ft (1.2 m)	Summer–fall
Hutchinsia alpina	Evergreen rock plant; well-drained cool soil	3-4 in (7.5-10 cm)	Summer
Iberis sempervirens	Evergreen, spreading; well-drained soil; sun or light shade	9 in (23 cm)	Spring–summer
Ipheion uniflorum	Bulbous, scented; well-drained soil; sun; shelter	4-6 in (10-15 cm)	Spring
Leontopodium alpinum	Rock plant; gritty soil; full sun	½-1 ft (15-30 cm)	Summer
Liatris scariosa 'White Spire'	Grassy clumps; moist soil; full sun	3 ft (90 cm)	Summer–fall
Lysimachia clethroides	Wide-spreading; moist soil; sun or shade	3 ft (90 cm)	Summer–fall
Macleaya cordata	Large lobed leaves; rich soil; sun or light shade	8 ft (2.4 m)	Summer
Nierembergia repens	Carpeting plant; well-drained soil; sun	2 in (5 cm)	Summer
Ornithogalum umbellatum	Bulb for naturalizing; well-drained soil; sun	6 in (15 cm)	Spring
Polygonatum spp.	Arching stems; moist acid soil; shade	2-6 ft (60-180 cm)	Spring–summer
Primula sieboldii 'Alba'	Bright green leaves; moist soil; sun or light shade	10 in (25 cm)	Late spring
Raoulia glabra	Carpeting evergreen; well-drained soil; sun	Prostrate	Spring
Rodgersia spp.	Foliage plants; moist, rich soil; light shade	3-6 ft (90-180 cm)	Summer
Sanguinaria canadensis	Rock plant; rich, well-drained soil; sun	6-8 in (15-20 cm)	Spring
Saxifraga spp. and cvs.	Evergreen rosettes; moist, well-drained soil; sun	1-18 in (2.5-45 cm)	Spring–summer
Silene vulgaris 'Plena'	Evergreen; any soil; sun or light shade	1-2 ft (30-60 cm)	Summer
Sisyrinchium striatum	Evergreen, grassy; rich soil; sun	1½ ft (45 cm)	Summer
Smilacina racemosa	Arching stems; rich, moist soil; shade	3 ft (90 cm)	Spring–summer
Symphytum grandiflorum	Ground-cover plant; any soil; sun or shade	1 ft (30 cm)	Early spring
Tiarella cordifolia	Semievergreen; rich, moist soil; cool shade	1 ft (30 cm)	Spring–summer
Veratrum californicum	Handsome leaves; moist soil; light shade	4-6 ft (1.2-1.8 m)	Summer

Yellow and orange flowers

Yellow is a cheerful, sunny color, often associated with spring flowers such as aconites, narcissi, primulas, and forsythias. However, it is also found in summer and fall gardens, as well as in the bright winter splashes of mahonias, winter jasmines, and witch hazels. As it is so close to green in the color spectrum, yellow harmonizes well with most foliage, especially soft green and gray; and yellow foliage itself should never be overlooked.

After white, yellow is the most eye-catching color in the garden. It is luminous and stands out distinctly at a distance, thus appearing to be closer than it really is. Perceived by the eye as a warm color, yellow varies from a pale pastel yellow to clear primrose, dusty sulfur to bright gold, and peach and apricot to orange-red, with many muted shades in between.

Yellow tones are ideal for creating single-color schemes in the garden, especially in lightly shaded areas. For maximum effect, plant yellow flowers in bold clumps rather than sprinkling them around in small patches. Some yellows, such as apricot and pale yellow-orange, lose their intensity next to clearer shades; instead, they are best placed in foliage settings.

The Compositae (daisy) family includes a vast range of yellow and orange flowers. There are also numerous other sources of yellow, including spring bulbs, many roses, dahlias, chrysanthemums, irises, and yarrows. It is also worth seeking out lesser-known yellow-flowered plants such as *Delphinium semibarbatum,* the showy yellow *Nicotiana glauca, Rhododendron luteum,* the gold-leaved Mexican orange *Choisya ternata* 'Sundance,' and *Clematis tangutica*, which bears rich yellow flowers that glow like lanterns in late summer and fall.

Gold and yellow Orange-gold honeysuckle arches over golden marjoram and Welsh poppies.

SHADES OF YELLOW

**Use yellow flowers and golden foliage
to create focal points in your garden or to bring
sunny hues to dark, shaded corners.**

When you introduce a single-color planting theme to a garden, it's important to consider all the qualities and characteristics of that color. This makes it easier for you to decide on an effective site for the planting — half the story of successful garden design.

For instance, yellow is perceived more quickly than other colors — it immediately attracts the eye. So all-yellow plantings are ideal for drawing attention to a particular feature in the garden or for creating focal points.

Because yellow flowers are luminous, they are perfect for cheering up dark, shady corners; creating deceptive vistas; and filling containers and beds around a patio where you spend time in the fading evening light.

In any all-yellow planting try to introduce different tones. There are many shades available, from soft cream through primrose, lemon, green-yellow, and butter, to rich gold and a dazzling intense orange. Such contrasting shades make the picture more interesting and create a sense of depth. For example, when pale yellow flowers such as verbascum grow alongside the warmer, more intense yellow of *Achillea,* the former tend to recede, giving the grouping the illusion of depth.

Combining species with different flower shapes and textures is another trick for making your yellow planting theme stimulating to the eye. A mass grouping of clear yellow goblet-shaped tulips with their satiny petals and packed clusters of golden wallflowers, all edged with sprays of basket-of-gold *(Aurinia saxatilis),* makes a very effective spring planting for an island bed.

To keep arrangements of yellow-flowered plants from becoming overpowering, temper them with a foil of fresh green foliage. This touch of green completes the scene without detracting from the excitement.

Yellow flowers are not the only way of introducing pools of sunlight to beds and borders. Golden- or yellow-leaved plants can be just as successful, either interspersed with green foliage or as echoes of yellow-flowered species. They have the advantage of a longer-lasting display than most flowers. Such evergreens as variegated holly and ivy, spindle tree, golden privet, and *Elaeagnus* ensure a splash of color in your garden throughout the year, even during winter.

▼ **Daisy yellow** In midsummer, the corner of a herbaceous border is bright with sunshine-yellow daisies backed by pale loosestrife *(Lysimachia punctata)* and golden double-flowered sunflowers *(Helianthus decapetalus).*

▼ **Yellow brooms** In May the Warminster broom *(Cytisus x praecox)* lets loose a cascade of creamy yellow blossoms. The yellow theme has already been set by the plants behind it — the fading flowers of *Forsythia suspensa* and *Ribes sanguineum* 'Album.'

▲ **Lemon-yellow and green** The flowerlike bracts of the shrubby evergreen *Euphorbia epithymoides* shine like bright yellow suns on late-spring days and reflect the sheen on the dwarf *Chamaecyparis pisifera* 'Golden Mop.'

◄ **Contrasting shapes and shades** In this simple but fascinating array of gold and yellow, the contrasting shapes of red-hot poker *(Kniphofia* hybrids) and the flat heads of *Achillea filipendulina* 'Gold Plate' form an impressive combination.

▼ **Waterside plants** Bright yellow spikes of *Lysimachia punctata* challenge the foamy green-yellow blooms of *Alchemilla mollis*, whose soft green leaves contrast in turn with the sword-shaped foliage of water iris.

◀ **Gold foliage** The cut-leaved golden elder *(Sambucus racemosa* 'Plumosa Aurea') has finely dissected golden-yellow foliage that opens pink-tinted in spring, before the upright clusters of creamy white flowers bloom. The leaves retain their color throughout the growing season, especially in light shade, and contrast with the plant's scarlet berries in late summer. A ground cover of golden lemon balm *(Melissa officinalis* 'Aurea') presents a similar look.

▼ **Bewitching in winter** The witch hazels are popular shrubs for the winter garden — especially *Hamamelis mollis* 'Pallida,' whose naked branches are crowded with scented sulfur-yellow flowers. Here it is underplanted with a variegated form of *Euonymus japonicus* and bright sweet box *(Sarcococca confusa).*

YELLOW AND GREEN

**Bring out the radiance of yellow and
golden flowers by placing them in the company
of green and yellow foliage.**

The many tints and shades of green form a perfect background for other colors. When combined with yellow — a component of green, together with blue — the result is a harmonious one. Yellow and gold are found not only in flowers but also in the variegated and all-yellow foliage of trees, shrubs, grasses, and perennials.

The long, lime-green catkins of the evergreen shrub *Garrya ellip-*

tica are highly decorative from early fall to late spring. For a delightful combination, try pairing this shrub with the yellow blooms and bare greenish stems of winter-flowering jasmine *(Jasminum nudiflorum)*. You might also underplant both with late-winter-blooming *Crocus flavus* and *Narcissus* 'February Gold.'

Several spurges have blends of green and yellow foliage and

flower bracts. One of the best is *Euphorbia epithymoides,* whose yellow bracts appear in mid- to late spring in a clump 1½ ft (45 cm) high. The fresh yellow leaves of Bowles' golden grass *(Milium effusum* 'Aureum') make an ideal color match and provide variety with their contrasting shape. Viridiflora tulips, such as 'Golden Artist,' which has golden yellow flowers and green splashes on fringed petals, could add the finishing touch.

For an evergreen late-spring combination in shade, start with the spurge *Euphorbia robbiae.* It has yellow-green bracts and narrow, dark green leaves, which provide contrast for the pale green, scalloped foliage of *Tellima grandiflora purpurea.* The latter is also green-flowered, although its foliage turns purple in the fall. To add brightness, plant *Tolmiea menziesii* 'Variegata' with its primrose-yellow speckled leaves.

During the summer *Sisyrinchium striatum* has erect irislike pale green leaves almost 1 ft (30 cm) tall and creamy yellow flowers on spikes that rise twice as high. For foliage contrast, try *Santolina virens,* which has rich green, divided leaves and bright yellow flowers in midsummer. Complete the group by planting the golden yellow starlike flowers and green serrated leaves of alkaline-hating *Chrysogonum virginianum.*

Too much yellow or green can become dull; to prevent monotony, choose different-shaped flowers in varying tones of the same color. In late summer and early fall, the golden yellow daisies of *Helenium autumnale* are eye-catching if backed by the scented yellowish-green flower plumes and jagged green leaves of mugwort *(Artemisia lactiflora).*

◀ **Gold and green foliage** The ribbonlike sheaves of foliage belonging to the golden-variegated grass *Hakonechloa macra* 'Aureola' provide a startling contrast when mingled with the broad, glossy green and deeply veined leaves of *Hosta sieboldiana.*

▲ **Yellow poppies** Yellow or orange Welsh poppies *(Meconopsis cambrica)* take on a luminous quality against a background of the variegated dogwood *(Cornus alba* 'Elegantissima'). Welsh poppies, which are short-lived but seed themselves freely, flower in early summer to early fall in zones 6 to 9.

◀ **Winter sunshine** The glossy-leaved evergreen *Mahonia japonica* is one of the pearls of the winter garden. Its fragrant lemon-yellow flower sprays appear as early as January in zone 8. Here they are joined in early spring by the lime-green flower clusters of Corsican hellebore *(Helleborus lividus corsicus)* rising above an underplanting of snowdrops, pale blue *Iris reticulata*, and creeping ivy *(Hedera helix* 'Glacier').

◄ **Soft harmony** Statuesque, pale yellow double-flowered hollyhocks *(Alcea)* are contrasted with the 6 ft (1.8 m) weaving stems of the graceful grass *Stipa gigantea*. A pompon-flowered cultivar of the thin-leaf sunflower *(Helianthus decapetalus)* repeats the double-flowered theme with golden blooms at the lower level. In the foreground, the foliage of a golden-leaved privet *(Ligustrum ovalifolium* 'Aureum') is also yellow and green.

▼ **Primrose yellow** In late spring the magnificent trusses of *Rhododendron* 'Goldsworth Yellow' open from apricot-pink buds into pale primrose-yellow blooms. This plant towers above the elegant stems of Solomon's seal *(Polygonatum)*, whose white bells hang above a matching front planting of white-edged *Hosta crispula*. By fall, the hostas' foliage will mellow to a soft yellow.

▲ **Buttery yellow** If planted at intervals from early spring to midsummer, gladioli hybrids will furnish spikes of glorious yellow until frost arrives in the North. In the South they may be planted and harvested all winter, too.

▼ **Yellow fringes** The fringecup (*Tellima grandiflora*) provides an evergreen ground cover of bright green maplelike leaves. In late spring and summer, slender spikes of bell-shaped flowers rise up stiffly in streaks of pale yellow above the green foliage.

▲ **Shady companions** With their architectural form, attractive foliage, and long-lasting bracts, the perennial spurges are wonderful elements in a garden. The semievergreen *Euphorbia characias* forms clumps, 3 ft (90 cm) high and wide, of narrow blue-green leaves. In late spring and early summer it is topped with huge heads of brown-eyed, lime-green inflorescenses that gradually change to sulfur-yellow. In spite of its Mediterranean origin, this spurge does well in light shade and is useful for brightening dull corners. Here it is combined with a gold-variegated ivy *(Hedera)*.

YELLOW AND ORANGE

To create lively arrangements, mix pale yellow with bright orange, then offset them with fresh green foliage.

Few gardeners can resist the temptation to incorporate yellow and orange into their gardens. These colors are bright and cheery, they clamor for attention, and many attractive species come in these hues.

Planted separately, though, yellow and orange have their drawbacks. Pale yellow can look rather cool and even white at twilight, and in bright sun, it often appears to be drained of color. Orange, on the other hand, is warm but lacks the luminosity of yellow, failing to stand out in poor light. However, if you plant them both together, each color appears to make up for the other's shortcomings, forming a satisfactory partnership. Midgreen foliage is the perfect accompaniment for such bright colors, bringing a touch of coolness to the display.

Good arrangements can be designed using totally different plants, but designs centered on a particular species are also attractive. Many species now come in both yellow and orange varieties. If you're planning a bed of annuals, consider using French marigolds, nasturtiums, wallflowers, and gazanias. When it comes to perennials, there are euphorbias, montebretias, and heleniums, while the choice of shrubs includes potentillas, azaleas, barberries, firethorns, rockroses, and helianthemums.

▲ **Perfect partners** In light shade, the cheery little orange Welsh poppies *(Meconopsis cambrica* 'Aurantiaca') nestle happily beneath 3 ft (90 cm) spikes of an unusual creamy yellow foxglove *(Digitalis grandiflora).*

▼ **Sunny colors** An eye-catching picture is created simply by planting mixed orange and yellow nasturtiums *(Tropaeolum majus* 'Alaska Hybrids'). They clamber in full sun and poor soil, blaring their bright trumpets over marbled leaves.

▲ Fall glow The evergreen firethorns are some of the most accommodating garden shrubs. In summer they are wreathed in great airy clusters of creamy white hawthornlike flowers — though without the hawthorn's delicious scent. In the fall, varieties like *Pyracantha* 'Orange Glow' and 'Soleil d'Or' are decorated with long-lasting, brilliantly colored berries. They will grow in any soil and against walls of any exposure.

◄ Summer exotics Sheltered by a wall, the orange-red blooms of purple-leaved *Canna* 'Wyoming' glow dramatically in late-summer sun. In front they are contrasted, in form and hue, with dainty apricot-yellow flowers of montebretia (*Crocosmia x crocosmiiflora* 'Solfatare'). A deep yellow bedding dahlia balances these two extremes of the yellow color range.

◄ **Summer annuals** Yellow and orange annuals create a profusion of dazzling color during the height of summer. Tall, graceful cosmos, with feathery leaves, tower at the back in a range of yellow and orange shades from the mixture *Cosmos sulphureus* 'Bright Lights.' In front is a bushy edging of low-growing *Tagetes tenuifolia*, one of the many marigolds that range from yellow to orange.

Such sunny combinations need to be tempered by fresh green foliage. Here, annual summer cypresses *(Kochia scoparia)*, whose symmetrical mounds of light green leaves turn red in fall, are the perfect companion.

▶ **Spring carpets** A bed of polyanthus primulas in pale yellow, apricot, and orange is edged with an unusual tawny-colored variety of basket-of-gold *(Aurinia saxatilis)* — 'Dudley Neville.' The tulips at the back of the bed are the tall Darwin hybrids 'Beauty of Apeldoorn,' with creamy yellow petals overlaid with orange. Their lovely colors are perfectly matched by the shorter 'General de Wet' tulips, golden-orange and stippled with scarlet.

◄ **Goldenrods** In late summer and early fall, the yellow flowers of *Solidago* weave fluffy clusters at the back of many borders. Their airy form is given substance and their pale color provided with depth by clumps of sneezeweed *(Helenium autumnale)*. The daisylike flowers of the sneezeweed have prominent color-contrasting centers and are available in a range of colors including shades of yellow and orange, from pure sun-yellow to deep mahogany-orange and fiery reds.

► **Orange and yellow**
In late spring two euphorbias make an ideal marriage: the taller *Euphorbia griffithii* 'Fireglow' flaunts fiery orange bracts next to demure, bright yellow *Euphorbia epithymoides.* The small poached-egg flower *(Limnanthes douglasii)*, with its scented primroselike flowers of deep yellow edged with white, stands nearby. Although an annual, it self-seeds to reappear year after year.

YELLOW AND BLUE

Yellow and blue pairings are always successful — the contrast between warm yellow and cooler blue is eye-catching.

Yellow and blue are most often thought of as a spring combination. Who can resist a striking mixture of low-growing primroses with grape hyacinths or scillas — especially when they appear under deciduous trees that do not yet have their leaves? Or the equally attractive taller combinations of daffodils and bluebells?

The beauty of this color combination, though, is that it is just as successful in summer and fall. When petunias, salvias, peonies, and roses are flaunting their brilliant, hot shades of red and purple, yellows and blues seem refreshing and cooling. Try to experiment with this mixture by planting golden yarrow, doronicum, or goldenrod with blue delphiniums, bellflowers, or lobelias.

In the fall a pairing of misty blue *Caryopteris* with yellow dahlias is most effective. Even in late winter there's a delightful combination — yellow winter aconites interspersed with clumps of deep blue *Iris reticulata*.

When planning your color scheme, don't forget to consider the ultimate height of the plant, how much it will spread, and the flowering time of each species.

▲ **Summer annuals** Bright yellow and white poached-egg flowers *(Limnanthes douglasii)* mix with baby blue-eyes *(Nemophila menziesii)* at the edges of a cheerful low border.

▼ **Yellow foam** Yellow-green sprays of lady's-mantle *(Alchemilla mollis)* tumble among cool summer blues, such as perennial veronicas, lobelias, larkspurs, linums, and polemoniums.

◀ **Late-summer sheen** In this bed the bright daisy flowers of the 4 ft (1.2 m) tall coneflower *(Rudbeckia)* contrast perfectly in color and form with the cool blue spiny heads of the globe thistle *(Echinops ritro)*. The globe thistle is an excellent plant to cut and dry for indoor winter decoration.

▲ **Spring carpets** Bright sun in late spring brings out the clear colors of yellow lily-flowered tulips rising above a carpet of blue forget-me-nots. The biennial forget-me-nots seed themselves freely — sometimes in places where they are not wanted. Thin them out once flowering has finished.

▶ **Creeping yellows** At the height of summer, the shrubby St.-John's-wort *(Hypericum olympicum)* trails its golden flowers over a rock garden, close to the sprawling stems of bright blue speedwell *(Veronica prostrata)*. On the left a clump of golden flax *(Linum flavum)* is more restrained.

YELLOW AND PURPLE

Putting yellow and purple together is a daring color move, requiring careful choice of plants. When successful, the match can be stunning.

When purple flowers are blended with similarly colored blooms, the effect is muted and soft. But if yellow flowers or leaves are added, a sense of excitement is brought to the scene. However, there is a catch; if both colors are quite brilliant — for instance, deep purple and rich yellow — the arrangement can become jarring rather than enticing. Instead, match bright yellows with subdued purples or soft, subtle yellows with bright purples.

In early spring to midspring the bare branches of forsythia are thickly covered with yellow bell-like flowers. Cool this overabundance by underplanting clumps of large-flowered purple crocuses. 'Pickwick,' for example, has pale lilac petals feathered with stripes of a deeper color.

At the same time of the year, clusters of creamy yellow English primrose (*Primula vulgaris*) mingle well with the purplish petals of dog's-tooth violet (*Erythronium dens-canis*) — these two woodland lovers are at home in a shaded setting. As both plants are low-growing, add height with the 1 ft (30 cm) tall wild daffodil *Narcissus pseudonarcissus*.

Erysimum 'Bowles' Mauve' is a sub-shrubby perennial wallflower with rosettes of gray-green leaves and lilac flowers from early summer onward. It needs a well-drained, sunny site and makes an excellent partner for the low-growing golden sage (*Salvia officinalis* 'Icterina'), whose leaves are marked with primrose and gold.

Another sun-loving shrub is the 4 ft (1.2 m) evergreen Jerusalem sage (*Phlomis fruticosa*). It has hairy, wrinkled gray-green leaves and hooded yellow flowers that appear during the summer. For contrast in flower color and shape, use it as a background for *Hebe* 'Autumn Glory' This plant is about half the height of Jerusalem sage and has oval, glossy green leaves, with mauve to purplish flowers during summer and fall. The hebe also looks good with the equally long-flowering *Potentilla fruticosa* 'Goldfinger' — a twiggy, compact shrub of the same height as the hebe, but with deep yellow flowers and small divided leaves.

Several hostas have flowers in pale lilacs and purples. 'Tall Boy' has green heart-shaped leaves with flowering stems up to 4 ft (1.2 m) high. The lobed leaves of the flowering currant (*Ribes sanguineum*), in its yellow-leaved form 'Brocklebankii,' provide a pleasing backdrop for the hosta's violet flowers.

New York asters (*Aster novi-belgii*) come into their own in early fall. There are several varieties with purplish-blue flowers, such as the 3 ft (90 cm) double-flowered 'Ada Ballard.' A yellow-bloomed variety of the tall hybrid dahlias, with richly colored flowers that open into neat, tight balls, makes a pleasing companion.

◄ **Climbing duet** In early summer and midsummer the bright yellow flowers of the climbing variety of the semidouble rose 'Allgold' are a delightful contrast to the deep lavender flowers of *Clematis* 'Lasurstern.'

▲ **Evening primrose** At the front of a border, the evening primrose *(Oenothera missouriensis)* opens its satiny, pale yellow flowers during the day as well as at dusk. It blooms throughout summer. Here it is attractively combined with a much taller, glossy-leaved *Eryngium,* whose evergreen foliage is marked with silvery veins that match the bracts around its purplish-blue flower globes.

◄ **Yellow yarrows** The large flat-topped heads of yarrows *(Achillea)* are popular choices for a herbaceous border. They give substance to more fleeting flowers and bloom without any fuss throughout summer and early fall. *Achillea filipendulina* 'Gold Plate,' at a height of 4 ft (1.2 m), is best sited at the back of a border, where its deep yellow flower heads can contrast with the fragrant purple clusters of *Verbena bonariensis.* Although the verbena is not hardy north of zone 7, it seeds itself freely and seedlings appear each spring.

◄ **Sunny spring** The lovely bulbous *Iris bucharica* creates stunning focal points in large rock gardens during late spring. Carrying up to six flowers on each of its 1½ ft (45 cm) stems, rising between glossy gray-green leaves, the bright yellow and creamy white blooms create patches of sunshine on the cloudiest day, especially when viewed against a dark background. A clump of the elegant pasqueflower *(Anemone pulsatilla)* provides contrast in shape, color, and foliage, with large, soft goblet-shaped purple blooms nodding above ferny leaves.

◄ **Golden rain** The brilliant yellow hanging trusses, up to 2 ft (60 cm) long, of *Laburnum* x *watereri* 'Vossii' soften the intensity of a violet underplanting. Ornamental onions are spectacular early-summer border plants, but the fiery color of the large flower globes on *Allium rosenbachianum* requires careful place-ment when teamed with softer-toned inhabitants.

▼ **Gentle summer tints** A harmonious blend of soft colors creates a restful yet pleasing border of pale yellows and lavender-blues. Silvery purple pansies in the front complement the giant bellflower *(Campanula latifolia)*, whose purple-blue bells borrow warmth from fluffy, pale yellow dwarf goldenrods (such as *Solidago* 'Golden Dwarf' or 'Golden Thumb'). The golden daisies of *Inula hookeri* and tall-stemmed holly-hocks of pale primrose-yellow paint even more delicate shades.

▲ **Lighten up** The clear yellows and oranges of Welsh poppies *(Meconopsis cambrica)* lighten the deep magenta of black-eyed *Geranium psilostemon*, which flowers during the summer.

▲ **Cascades of purple** Trained along wire supports, the large purple flowers of late-summer-flowering Clematis 'The President' tumble among the branches of a dogwood (Cornus alba 'Spaethii'). Its gold-variegated leaves add luster to the sea of purple and are reinforced by a low-growing shrubby cinquefoil (Potentilla fruticosa) which has delicate primrose-yellow blooms.

▲ **Winter willows** The thick black buds that dot the Japanese willow (Salix gracilistyla melanostachys) through the winter months shed their shells at the first thaw to reveal velvety crimson-jet catkins. A month later these burst into showers of golden pollen. Only one plant — golden trumpet daffodils — can match their splendor.

◀ **Gold dust** Flowering profusely from early spring and into summer, purple aubrietas are easy to grow in sunny rock gardens and on banks and walls. An excellent companion is the adaptable Alyssum montanum 'Mountain Gold,' whose clusters of tiny golden stars bob through the sea of purple blooms and dark green foliage.

YELLOW THROUGH THE YEAR

**Yellow shades match the sun, from pale
lemon in winter, through gold in spring and summer,
to the fiery orange of an autumn sunset.**

During the bleakest months of the year, yellow flowers bring the promise of spring. Even the grayest day is brightened by the sight of a winter jasmine against a wall or a small clump of aconites lifting their yellow faces above fallen winter-brown leaves. Early narcissi — both the shy little trumpets of 'Peeping Tom' or the hoop petticoats of *Narcissus bulbocodium* — are forerunners of the splashes of yellow, gold, and orange to come from spring daffodils, crocuses, tulips, and irises, and from bright yellow forsythia and the golden buttercups of *Kerria japonica.*

Yellow turns to gold with the flowering brooms and barberries, with primroses and cowslips, erigerons and globeflowers *(Trollius europaeus)*. Late spring is the season for the magnificent blooms of rhododendrons and azaleas, such as the creamy yellow *Rhododendron* 'Goldfort' and the rich gold of 'Narcissiflorum' azaleas. Summer is heralded by early roses; dainty, bright 'Harison's Yellow' and the heavy-scented pale golden blooms of 'Frühlingsgold.' There are golden laburnums and lilacs *(Syringa vulgaris* 'Primrose'), with potentillas and hypericums below them. And you can fill your beds with tall ligularias and pale yellow mulleins, peonies, and yarrows *(Achillea)* in many shades.

Fall brings rudbeckias and heleniums, dahlias and chrysanthemums, with tall, double-flowered *Helianthus* and the creamy yellow funnels of *Kirengeshoma palmata.* Other fall treats include the bright hues of marigolds and self-sown clumps of California poppies *(Eschscholzia californica)*, gold and orange leaf tints, and clusters of fruit and berries on crab apples, bittersweet, and firethorns.

▼ **Late-summer sun** Clear yellow montebretias *(Crocosmia x crocosmiiflora)* form the centerpiece in this late-summer scene. Their long, thin dark green leaves are echoed in a tall clump of green-and-yellow variegated New Zealand flax *(Phormium tenax* 'Variegatum').

◄ **Summer blaze** The impressive
orange trumpets of a 'Mid-Century
Hybrid' lily reach out from a sea
of bright yellow summer-blooming
Lysimachia punctata. The yellow-
green flowers and soft foliage of
Alchemilla mollis (lady's-mantle)
cool the fire of this grouping.

▼ **Green borders** Here, lady's-mantle
(*Alchemilla mollis*) is ideal for edging
beds and in flower arrangements.
Throughout the summer the leafy clumps
are topped with billowing sprays of
long-lasting yellow-green flowers.

▲ Yellow summer border Clusters of golden marguerite *(Anthemis tinctoria)* with pale yellow daisy blooms mingle with robust Jerusalem sage *(Phlomis fruticosa)*, which embellishes the scene with its whorls of hooded golden yellow flowers.

▲ Orange and yellow
The intense orange *Geum* x *borisii* needs to be placed where it can receive the strong sun of midsummer. A group of tiny, bright yellow evening primroses *(Oenothera missouriensis)* provides the perfect cooling effect, further helped by a backdrop of the elegant dark green foliage of stinking hellebore *(Helleborus foetidus)*.

◄ Autumn layers Not all red-hot pokers are red. Varieties like *Kniphofia* 'Gold Mine' or 'Primrose Beauty' can add eye-catching vertical interest to an early fall scene. They are accompanied by the brown-centered, golden-orange daisy flowers of *Helenium autumnale* and backed by the crimson-purple spikes of *Salvia* x *superba*. In the foreground the flat heads of *Sedum* 'Autumn Joy' are still yellow-green.

▲ **Drops of gold** In early fall the evergreen shrub *Bupleurum fruticosum* becomes an airy cloud bank of delicate fennel-yellow flowers gathered in rounded heads. Prized by flower arrangers, these blooms also provide a graceful background for the primrose-yellow flowers of marguerites *(Argyranthemum frutescens)*.

▶ **Yellow goblets** Fall-flowering *Sternbergia lutea* opens its waxy yellow goblets wide to the touch of the late-summer sun. Native to scorched Mediterranean scrubland, these small bulbs revel in warmth and shelter along with other inhabitants of that region, such as silver-gray lavender *(Lavandula)* and semi-evergreen *Euphorbia characias wulfeni* with its blue-gray leaf whorls.

◀**Autumn mists** Set against a background of hazy silver-gray *Artemisia absinthium* 'Lambrook Silver,' groups of yellow, gold, and bronze chrysanthemums bring color to a fall border. These plants reflect the slanting rays of a lowering sun and the tints in fall foliage, but their radiance is extinguished with the first touch of frost.

▼ **Winter sun** In the pale sunshine of late winter, tiny winter aconites (*Eranthis hyemalis*) spread their lemon-yellow flower cups above tufts of pale green leaves. They carpet the ground beneath the bare coral-red stems of *Cornus alba* 'Sibirica.' On the left, the purplish stems of a shrubby willow (*Salix irrorata*) are overlaid with white bloom. The closely set catkins are about to burst at any moment.

▲ **Winter curios** The spiraling and twisted shoots of the corkscrew hazel (*Corylus avellana* 'Contorta') are particularly noticeable in their bare winter profile. Early in the year, yellow catkins droop from every curious bend and angle to shed their pollen over an under-planting bright with color from *Crocus* 'Golden Bunch' and clumps of little blue *Iris histrioides*.

▼ **Winter into spring** The evergreen Corsican hellebore (*Helleborus lividus corsicus*) is variably hardy, opening its huge clusters of lime-green cuplike flowers in midwinter in mild climates and blooming on into summer at the northern edge of its range (zone 6). Typically, the thick, leathery leaves and stout flower stems come into their full glory at the same time that the little lungwort (*Pulmonaria officinalis*), with its spotted leaves and pinkish-purple blooms, begins to flower.

▲ **Golden summer**
In this pretty arrangement, the clear yellow flowers of the charming marguerite (*Argyranthemum frutescens*) 'Jamaica Primrose' are echoed by the fascinating gold-marked foliage of the South American herb *Iresine herbstii*.

◄ **First rose of summer**
Species roses — such as this cultivar of *Rosa ecae*, the incense rose (*R. primula*), or the Scotch rose (*R. spinosissima*) — open their clear yellow blossoms at least a month before hybrid teas. They are just in time to soften the hot orange of these wallflowers and complement the large lemon-yellow cups of the fleetingly beautiful *Paeonia mlokosewitschii*.

YELLOW AND ORANGE FLOWERS

	NAME	DESCRIPTION AND SITE	HEIGHT	SEASON
TREES AND SHRUBS	Berberis julianae	Evergreen; any soil; sun or light shade	6-10 ft (1.8-3 m)	Spring
	Campsis radicans 'Flava'	Deciduous climber; any soil; sun	30 ft (9 m)	Summer–fall
	Caragana arborescens	Deciduous; ordinary soil; sun	15-20 ft (4.5 -6 m)	Spring
	Chimonanthus praecox	Deciduous; ordinary soil; sun; wall shelter	10 ft (3 m)	Winter
	Colutea arborescens	Deciduous; any soil; sun	6-10 ft (1.8-3 m)	Summer–fall
	Cornus mas	Deciduous; ordinary soil; sun	20-25 ft (6-7.5 m)	Early spring
	Coronilla emerus	Deciduous; ordinary soil; sun; shelter	8 ft (2.4 m)	Spring
	Corylopsis spp.	Deciduous; moist acid soil; sun	5-10 ft (1.5-3 m)	Winter–spring
	Corylus avellana 'Contorta'	Deciduous; twisted stems and leaves; well-drained soil; sun	to 6 ft (1.8 m)	Winter
	Cytisus scoparius cvs.	Deciduous; any well-drained soil; sun	5-10 ft (1.5-3 m)	Late spring–summer
	Diervilla sessilifolia	Deciduous, wide-spreading; any soil; sun or shade	3-5 ft (90-150 cm)	Summer
	Enkianthus campanulatus cvs.	Deciduous; moist acid soil; sun or partial shade	6-15 ft (1.8-4.5 m)	Late spring
	Forsythia spp. and cvs.	Deciduous; any soil; sun	4-10 ft (1.2-3 m)	Spring
	Genista spp.	Deciduous; any soil; sun	2-4 ft (60-120 cm)	Late spring–summer
	Hamamelis spp. and cvs.	Deciduous; moist acid soil; sun; shelter	6-10 ft (1.8-3 m)	Winter
	Helianthemum nummularium cvs.	Evergreen; ordinary soil; sun	4-6 in (10-15 cm)	Summer
	Hypericum calycinum	Semievergreen; any soil; sun	1-1½ ft (30-45 cm)	Summer–fall
	Jasminum nudiflorum	Deciduous; ordinary soil; sun or partial shade	3-4 ft (90-120 cm)	Winter
	Kerria japonica	Deciduous; ordinary soil; sun or shade	6-8 ft (1.8-2.4 m)	Spring
	Koelreuteria paniculata	Deciduous; any soil; sun	30-40 ft (9-12 m)	Summer
	Laburnum spp.	Deciduous trees; moist, well-drained soil; sun/shade	12-20 ft (3.6-6 m)	Late spring
	Lindera benzoin	Deciduous; fall tints; moist, well-drained soil; light shade	8 ft (2.4 m)	Spring
	Lonicera sempervirens cvs.	Deciduous climbers; ordinary soil; sun or shade	15-20 ft (4.5-6 m)	Summer
	Magnolia 'Elizabeth'	Deciduous; moist, well-drained soil; sun	50 ft (15 m)	Spring
	Mahonia spp. and cvs.	Evergreen; moist, well-drained acid soil; light shade	3-10 ft (90-300 cm)	Winter
	Paeonia suffruticosa hybrids	Deciduous; rich, well-drained soil; sun; shelter	4-6 ft (1.2-1.8.m)	Spring–summer
	Potentilla fruticosa cvs.	Deciduous; any soil; sun	3 ft (90 cm)	Summer–fall
	Rhus aromatica 'Gro-Low'	Deciduous; good fall color; any soil; sun	2 ft (60 cm)	Spring
	Sophora japonica 'Regent'	Deciduous; well-drained soil; sun	to 50 ft (15 m)	Summer
	Spartium junceum	Deciduous; any soil; sun	8-10 ft (2.4-3 m)	Summer–fall
ANNUALS	Antirrhinum 'Floral Carpet Yellow'	Half-hardy; rich soil; sun or light shade	8 in (20 cm)	Summer–fall
	Argemone mexicana	Hardy; light soil; sun	3 ft (90 cm)	Summer
	Calceolaria hybrids	Half-hardy; acid soil; sun; shelter	12-15 in (30-38 cm)	Summer–fall
	Calendula officinalis cvs.	Hardy; any soil; sun or shade	1-2 ft (30-60 cm)	Spring–fall
	Celosia cristata cvs.	Half-hardy; moist, well-drained soil; sun; shelter	2 ft (60 cm)	Summer–fall
	Dimorphotheca sinuata cvs.	Half-hardy; light, well-drained soil; sun	4-12 in (10-30 cm)	Summer–fall
	Eschscholzia californica	Half-hardy; poor soil; sun	1 ft (30 cm)	Summer–fall
	Gazania hybrids	Half-hardy; light soil; sun	9 in (23 cm)	Summer–fall
	Helichrysum cvs.	Half-hardy; suitable for drying; light soil; sun	3-4 ft (90-120 cm)	Summer
	Layia platyglossa	Hardy; sandy soil; sun	1½ ft (45 cm)	Summer–fall
	Limnanthes douglasii	Hardy; any soil; sun	½-1 ft (15-30 cm)	Spring–summer
	Mentzelia lindleyi	Hardy; light soil; sun; shelter	1½ ft (45 cm)	Spring
	Petunia 'Summer Sun'	Half-hardy Multiflora; well-drained soil; sun	1 ft (30 cm)	Summer–fall
	Tagetes spp. and cvs.	Half-hardy; any soil; sun	½-3 ft (15-90 cm)	Summer–fall
	Thunbergia alata	Half-hardy climber; well-drained soil; sun; shelter	10 ft (3 m)	Summer–fall
	Tropaeolum majus cvs.	Hardy; well-drained soil; sun	9-15 in (23-38 cm)	Summer–fall
	Ursinia anethoides	Half-hardy, ferny foliage; light soil; sun	1½ ft (45 cm)	Summer–fall
	Venidium fastuosum	Half-hardy; light soil; sun	2 ft (60 cm)	Summer
	Zinnia spp. and cvs.	Half-hardy; well-drained soil; sun	1-3 ft (30-90 cm)	Summer–fall

PERENNIALS, BULBS, CORMS, AND TUBERS

NAME	DESCRIPTION AND SITE	HEIGHT	SEASON
Achillea spp. and hybrids	Ferny foliage; any soil; sun	3-4 ft (90-120 cm)	Summer
Aconitum 'Ivorine'	Handsome foliage; deep moist soil; partial shade	3 ft (90 cm)	Late spring–summer
Adonis amurensis	Fine leaves; any soil; sun or shade	9-15 in (23-38 cm)	Winter–spring
Allium moly	Bulbous; any well-drained soil; sun	1 ft (30 cm)	Late spring
Alstroemeria aurantiaca	Narrow leaves; well-drained soil; sun; shelter	2-3 ft (60-90 cm)	Summer
Anthemis tinctoria	Ferny foliage; well-drained soil; sun	2½ ft (75 cm)	Summer
Aurinia saxatilis	Persistent gray foliage; well-drained soil; sun	½-2 ft (15-60 cm)	Spring
Caltha palustris	Round, shiny leaves; very moist soil; sun or light shade	1 ft (30 cm)	Early spring
Centaurea macrocephala	Thistlelike; well-drained soil; sun	4 ft (1.2 m)	Summer
Chrysogonum virginianum	Dense bright green foliage; acid soil; sun or light shade	½-1 ft (15-30 cm)	Spring–fall
Coreopsis spp. and cvs.	Easy-growing; well-drained soil; sun	1-2 ft (30-60 cm)	Spring–summer
Corydalis lutea	Handsome leaves; any soil; sun or shade	1 ft (30 cm)	Spring–fall
Crocosmia hybrids	Sword-shaped leaves; well-drained soil; sun	2-2½ ft (60-75 cm)	Summer
Crocus spp. and cvs.	Well-drained soil; sun or light shade	3-5 in (7.5-12 cm)	Winter–spring
Digitalis grandiflora, D. lutea	Hairy leaves; moist soil; light shade	1-3 ft (30-90 cm)	Late spring–summer
Doronicum spp. and cvs.	Heart-shaped leaves; moist soil; light shade	8-36 in (20-90 cm)	Spring
Draba spp.	Evergreen, mound forming; well-drained soil; sun	1-4 in (2.5-10 cm)	Spring–early summer
Eranthis spp.	Tuberous; loamy soil; sun or light shade	4 in (10 cm)	Winter–spring
Eremurus stenophyllus	Imposing plants; well-drained soil; sun	4 ft (1.2 m)	Summer
Erigeron aurantiacus	Mat forming; moist, well-drained soil; sun or light shade	10 in (25 cm)	Summer
Erythronium tuolumnense	Clump forming; moist soil; light shade	9-12 in (23-30 cm)	Spring
Euphorbia spp.	Handsome foliage/bracts; well-drained soil; sun	2-4 ft (60-120 cm)	Spring–summer
Fritillaria imperialis	Bulbous; loamy, well-drained soil; sun or light shade	2-3 ft (60-90 cm)	Late spring
Gaillardia cvs.	Gray-green foliage; light, well-drained soil; sun	10-30 in (25-75 cm)	Summer–fall
Gentiana lutea	Whorls of veined leaves; rich, moist, well-drained soil; sun or light shade	to 5 ft (1.5 m)	Summer
Geum spp. and cvs.	Border and rock plants; rich soil; sun or light shade	½-1 ft (15-30 cm)	Spring–summer
Helenium autumnale cvs.	Branching; any soil; sun	4-6 ft (1.2-1.8 m)	Summer–fall
Helianthus spp. and cvs.	Perennials and annuals; any soil; sun	4-6 ft (1.2-1.8 m)	Summer–fall
Heliopsis helianthoides	Single and double cvs.; well-drained soil; sun	3-4 ft (90-120 cm)	Summer
Hemerocallis hybrids	Easy-growing; any soil; sun or light shade	3 ft (90 cm)	Spring–fall
Hieracium villosum	Rosette forming; gray foliage; any soil; sun	1 ft (30 cm)	Summer
Inula spp.	Rock and border plants; well-drained soil; sun	4-24 in (10-60 cm)	Summer–fall
Kirengeshoma palmata	Attractive foliage; rich, moist acid soil; light shade	3 ft (90 cm)	Late summer–fall
Kniphofia hybrids	Clump forming; well-drained soil; sun	2-6 ft (60-180 cm)	Summer
Ligularia spp.	Large-leaved; moist soil; light shade	3-6 ft (90-180 cm)	Summer
Lysimachia punctata	Easy-growing; moist soil; sun or light shade	1-2 ft (30-90 cm)	Summer
Meconopsis cambrica	Ferny leaves; any soil; sun or light shade	1½ ft (45 cm)	Summer–fall
Mimulus guttatus	Hardy; moist soil; sun or light shade	2 ft (60 cm)	Summer–fall
Oenothera spp.	Border and rock plants; well-drained soil; sun	4-36 in (10-90 cm)	Summer
Paeonia lactiflora cvs.	Handsome foliage; moist soil; sun or light shade	2-3 ft (60-90 cm)	Early summer
Papaver pyrenaicum	Finely cut foliage; gritty well-drained soil; sun	6 in (15 cm)	Summer
Ranunculus spp. and cvs.	Bright green leaves; moist soil; sun or shade	6-30 in (15-75 cm)	Spring–summer
Roscoea cautleoides	Sword-shaped leaves; moisture-retentive soil; sun or shade	1 ft (30 cm)	Summer
Rudbeckia spp. and cvs.	Spreading; any soil; sun	2-7 ft (60-210 cm)	Summer–fall
Sedum aizoon	Glossy foliage; well-drained soil; sun	1 ft (30 cm)	Summer
Solidago spp. and cvs.	Invasive; any soil; sun	3-6 ft (90-180 cm)	Summer–fall
Thermopsis spp.	Clump forming; any soil; sun or light shade	1-3 ft (30-90 cm)	Summer
Tigridia pavonia	Bulbous, half-hardy; well-drained soil; sun; shelter	16-18 in (40-45 cm)	Summer–fall
Trollius spp.	Ornamental foliage; moist soil; sun or light shade	1-2½ ft (30-75 cm)	Spring
Verbascum spp.	Imposing plants; well-drained soil; sun	to 4 ft (1.2 m)	Summer
Waldsteinia ternata	Evergreen and mat forming; moist soil; sun or light shade	4 in (10 cm)	Spring

Pink and red flowers

Pink is a soft and friendly color, often associated with the romance and charm of sweetly scented old-fashioned gardens, especially in spring and summer. It is the color of flowering cherries, primulas, and spring quinces, as well as roses, peonies, garden pinks, and sweet peas. It also appears among vibrant fall colors — in the warm shades of colchicums and nerines. Late winter brings vibrant displays of bright pink to the heather garden and, in the south, offers the unsurpassed beauty of clear pink as well as bright red camellia blooms.

Pink and red hues range from pink-tinged white and clear cotton candy, through rich cerise, to scarlet, crimson, and magenta, merging into shades of purple and blue. There are the dusky pinks of eupatoriums, the vivid scarlet of bedding salvias, the salmon or coral-red of honeysuckles, and the reddish brown of some fall sedums. The paler the shade of pink, the more luminous it appears, particularly against a dark background. On the other hand, dark pinks and hot reds seem to vanish as dusk falls and need the cooling effects of gray, silver, or blue-green foliage to help bring them back into focus.

Monochromatic pale pink arrangements can look sugary and dull. In bright sunshine, these shades are all but lost unless they are contrasted with stronger shades. To be effective, a planting design should include a different range of mixes and tints of the basic color. When planning a garden, take advantage of the wide variety of flower shapes, textures, heights, and growth patterns. To make the most of harmonizing hues and contrasting forms, set pale colors against slightly darker ones, rigid shapes against airy profiles, and silky petals against stiff bracts.

An abundance of roses Climbers and shrub roses jostle in glorious summer colors.

PINK PERFECTION

**Pink flowers add a subtle
elegance to any garden — an effect that is
often enhanced by foliage color.**

In distinct contrast to warm yellows and cool blues, shades of pink generate a soft and nostalgic atmosphere — the essence of the old-fashioned cottage garden.

Pastel pinks glow in evening light, when darker hues are disappearing into the shadows. Lighter shades appear deeper when integrated with silvery white foliage, redder when seen against greens, and more vivid among grays. By day, pinks are less eye-catching than more intense colors, but they help soften the impact of bold architectural plants.

Many pink flowers are exceptionally beautiful when they are seen close up. There may be finely divided petals that provide a lacy, soft texture, a center of golden stamens that adds luster, or delicate traces of purple veins that enhance the primary color.

In late winter from zone 8 southward, camellias add color to an otherwise bleak landscape. Although frosts and snow cause pale colors to fade into obscurity, the glossy green leaves of camellias provide the perfect background for their stunning flowers.

Heralding spring, flowering almonds burst forth with soft pink flowers before there is even a hint of greenery. With flowering cherries, the impact of the pink flowers is heightened by purplish or bronze foliage. Underplantings of the pink-flowered *Anemone blanda* and groupings with viburnums complete the picture.

Middle to late spring is often associated with the vivacious yellows and reds of daffodils and tulips, but there are many pink flowers, too. The tuliplike flowers of the saucer magnolia — as well

▲ **Old-fashioned pinks** The deliciously scented bourbon rose 'Mme. Isaac Pereire' bears huge cerise-pink blooms in early summer and again in fall. It is accompanied by pink hybrids of *Paeonia lactiflora*.

▼ **Cottage-garden charm** This all-pink theme combines many shades; including a ring of *Aubriet deltoidea*, containers of rhododendrons and evergreen azaleas, and tall columbines (*Aquilegia* x *hybrida*).

as sprays of pink deciduous aza-leas and clumps of the rosy dwarf Russian almond *(Prunus tenella)* — look striking alongside masses of woodland primulas, dog's-tooth violets, and bergenias. For a beau-tiful climbing backdrop, choose *Clematis montana* varieties such as 'Elizabeth' or 'Rubens,' or *C. macropetala* 'Markham's Pink.'

Summer brings many and var-ied pink effects — from hazy seas of *Geranium endressii* or *Gyp-sophila paniculata* 'Rosy Veil' to the statuesque elegance of *Cleome* 'Rose Queen' or perennial fox-gloves *(Digitalis × mertonensis)*. Silver-leaved plants peak in sum-mer and are livened by sharper pink shades — some of the petu-nias, for instance.

From late summer to fall, warm tones of orange and bronze pre-dominate, yet there are surprises. Belladonna lilies *(Amaryllis belladonna)*, *Cyclamen hederifoli-um*, fall-flowering crocuses *(Cro-cus kotschyanus*, for example), and colchicums are all excellent for underplanting in groups or informal clusters — perhaps under the reddish-purple foliage of *Euonymus hamiltonianus* (var. *sieboldianus)*.

▲ Autumn pinks
Single-flowered, pale pink spray chrysanthemums backed by tall, massed clumps of deeper pink Japanese anemones *(Anemone × hybrida)* provide welcome relief in fall borders, when fiery orange and bronze colors usually predominate.

◄ Shades of pink
In September and October, the South African *Nerine bowdenii* raises tall, leafless stems topped with huge, elegant clusters of satiny, glowing-pink flowers. The bare stems are concealed by clumps of deep rose-pink cornflowers *(Centaurea hypoleuca* 'John Coutts'), with gray-green, deeply divided foliage, and by the pale pink goblets of the autumn crocus *(Colchicum autumnale)*. Complementing the fall scene is a variegated *Fuchsia magellanica*, 4 ft (1.2 m) tall, which drips pink and purple blooms from its gray, green, and pink foliage.

▲ **Pink and white** February daphne *(Daphne mezereum)* begins to flower in late winter, wreathing its branches in scented blooms of rose to purple-pink. An early-spring combination might include *Crocus sieberi* 'Firefly' and white and pink *Anemone blanda*.

▲ **Pink and scarlet** The yarrow *(Achillea millefolium)* is the parent of many border plants, including the cherry-pink 'Cerise Queen,' whose large flower heads contrast well with its feathery green foliage. At the height of summer, this cultivar brings splashes of bright color to herbaceous borders. It is particularly vivid in the company of these taller hybrid penstemons, whose tubular flowers are vibrant crimson-scarlet.

◄ **Pink and peach** The 'Excelsior' strain of the common foxglove *(Digitalis purpurea)* includes a range of colors — pink, apricot, peach, and white. The 5 ft (1.5 m) flower stems are completely at home in any type of garden. Here the spikes of bell-shaped blooms tower above deep pink rugosa roses and the small red flower clusters of an evergreen escallonia.

▶ **Pink annuals** Many strains of annuals and biennials are sold in mixed colors, but others are available in single shades. Snapdragons *(Antirrhinum)* and flowering tobacco *(Nicotiana)* both come in named color selections. Here, rose-pink snapdragons and cerise nicotianas are arranged around a perennial, the pink-flowered yarrow *Achillea millefolium* 'Red Beauty.'

▼ **Red as roses** In the late spring, a large-scale planting of evergreen rhododendrons is smothered with huge clusters of reddish-pink blooms. Their color and shape are repeated in the wide-spreading but smaller-flowered azalea *(Rhododendron obtusum* 'Amoenum'). The same stunning color effect can be achieved in small gardens with dwarf rhododendron and azalea hybrids.

PINK AND WHITE

**Delicate combinations of pink and white
flowers increase their visual impact when combined
with bold, fresh green foliage plants.**

The combination of pink and white is very lively and popular with gardeners. During the day, pink shows up well in the diffused light of overcast days; toward dusk, white brings freshness and clarity to the garden.

Green foliage, whether it is evergreen or deciduous, and subtle green flowers can play an important role in strengthening pink and white pairings. You can create unique displays by experimenting with various shades and tints, as well as textures and shapes. Bring brightness to the winter garden, for example, by planting groups of pink and white winter heath *(Erica carnea)* around narrow conifers whose foliage ranges from deepest green to blue-green and golden green.

For spring arrangements, plant white narcissi beneath a pink-flowering cherry tree. On a more intimate scale, the trout lily *(Erythronium* 'White Beauty'), with its mottled green foliage, pairs well with *Anemone blanda* 'Pink Star,' which has lobed, deeply cut leaves that accentuate the starry form of its flowers. The large, leathery leaves of *Bergenia* 'Silberlicht' offer a striking contrast to the other plants' foliage while its silvery pink blooms complement the other plants' flowers.

White roses, such as the glossy-leaved 'Iceberg,' look even better when underplanted with the deeply cut midgreen leaves and pink flowers of *Geranium endressii* 'Wargrave Pink.' Use the climber *Actinidia kolomikta* to introduce vertical interest in the rear. Its unusual foliage continues the pretty color theme.

In the fall, combine the lilac-pink goblets of *Colchicum autumnale* with the pink and white forms of *Cyclamen hederifolium*. For ground cover, use the bold, variegated green and white foliage of ivy *(Hedera helix* 'Eva'). Such color combinations introduce a fresh note to the typical oranges and golds of fall gardens.

▼ **Pink, green, and white** In the spring this corner of a woodland garden is a joyful combination. The tall, fluffy white plumes of *Smilacina racemosa* seem to shimmer against the tiny blooms of the red-flowered broom , pink rhododendrons, and green conifers.

▲ Spring companions In late spring, the pink-flowered thrift *(Armeria maritima)* offsets the dainty white sprays of St. Bernard's lily *(Anthericum liliago)*. Both have grassy leaves that offer an attractive color contrast.

▼ Shady summer borders The flat-headed pink blooms of *Spiraea japonica* are the centerpiece of this planting. White feverfew *(Tanacetum parthenium)* lends brightness, and broad-leaved hostas and sword-shaped iris foliage frame the mixture.

▲ Ornamental onions The large *Allium* family includes the tall *A. sphaerocephalum*, with its unusual purple-pink globes. Here they are combined with white clusters of *A. neapolitanum* and the rose-colored *A. ostrowskianum*.

▶ Pink accents The fingered leaves of a Japanese maple provide a handsome backdrop for the tall pink spikes of knotweed *(Polygonum bistorta* 'Superba') rising above white *Argyranthemum frutescens*, white-variegated hostas, and red potentillas.

▲ **Winter cheer** In late winter this little pastel-colored group creates an unforgettable picture. The soft pink cups of the Lenten rose *(Helleborus orientalis)* rise above the broad, spear-shaped glossy green leaves of *Arum italicum italicum*, which are marbled with cream and gray. In their shadow, snowdrops *(Galanthus nivalis)* gently nod their white bells.

▲ **Summer tints** An informal corner of this herbaceous border is filled with old-fashioned herbs. In the back are the branched spikes of the 4 ft (1.2 m) tall biennial clary *(Salvia sclarea)*, which is closely packed with pinkish-white flowers.

The pink theme is repeated in the large, soft flowers of the peony 'Bowl of Beauty' and in the smaller cerise blooms of cranesbill *(Geranium psilostemon)*. The entire airy group is given form and substance by the enormous, deeply divided, aromatic green leaves of *Angelica archangelica* rising from a froth of white feverfew *(Tanacetum parthenium)*.

◄ **Sweet alyssum** Correctly known as *Lobularia maritima*, this little annual spreads far and wide during the summer. The white tones are echoed in the double-flowered form of *Tanacetum parthenium*, whose buttonlike blooms stand above fernlike foliage, and in the bowl-shaped flowers of another annual, *Lavatera trimestris* 'Mont Blanc.'

At the rear of this planting are the pinks and whites of the flowering tobacco *(Nicotiana)*, freshened by the subtle coloring of the cultivar 'Lime Green.'

◀ **Summer tapestry** One of the joys of annuals is their long-lasting displays of color. Candytuft *(Iberis umbellata)* is deservedly popular, spreading its blend of white, pink, lavender, and pale mauve flower heads in a color tapestry. Here it is interwoven with the similarly colored *Clarkia unguiculata,* providing an eye-catching contrast of form with its tall, slender spikes.

▼ **Late-summer symphony** By August the herbaceous border may look shabby where early perennials have died back. Annuals fill such gaps to perfection, bringing a new freshness to the permanent occupants. The profuse blooms of mallow *(Lavatera trimestris),* with their wide rosy funnels, mingle with heavily scented, pastel-hued flowering tobacco plants *(Nicotiana alata)* and the deeper pink heads of perennial *Phlox paniculata.*

Late-summer harmony Pink *Dicentra eximia* blends with blue lavender and *Echinops ritro.*

PINK AND BLUE

**Bright or misty blues and dark or
pale pinks form combinations offering subtle
contrasts and muted harmony.**

When blue and red are placed side by side, they often clash, striking a jarring note. However, if pink is substituted for red, a pairing with blue becomes not only possible but highly pleasing. These two colors harmonize and at the same time offer sufficient contrast to retain individual interest. This point is well illustrated in a typical flower bed arrangement using pale pink tulips among a sea of forget-me-nots, (which is preferable to scarlet tulips among crisp blue muscaris).

The deep blue of veronicas and some irises and delphiniums can be somber, but this mood is easily lifted if you grow pale pink flowers alongside. The luminescence of pale pink also makes the blue stand out in fading light.

Creating attractive plant combinations is more than simply choosing the colors. Quantity is also important. The rule of thumb is that there should be larger clusters of the softer color than of the stronger one. Large groupings of intense color can overwhelm the eye and draw attention away from other aspects of the garden.

Remember that visual appeal is increased by using contrasting forms. For example, set the frothy blue flowers of ceanothus against the bold pink blooms of a climbing rose such as 'Pink Perpetué.' Or in moist, semishaded conditions, combine the rosy candelabra-flowered *Primula pulverulenta* hybrids with the saucer-shaped blooms of the Himalayan blue poppy *(Meconopsis betonicifolia)*.

▲ **Midsummer partners** The pink bowl-shaped blossoms of this *Sidalcea malviflora* form a soft foil for the metallic blues of spiky *Eryngium* x *oliveranum.*

▼ **Midsummer mists** The impact of these rich blue sprays of *Anchusa azurea* is toned down by a deep pink peony, pink and rose-red foxgloves *(Digitalis purpurea),* and stately spikes of lavender-blue delphiniums.

▶ **Summer annuals** Half-hardy begonias *(Begonia semperflorens-cultorum)* flower incessantly from late spring until frost. With their glossy green or purple leaves and deep pink flowers, they make handsome low-growing companions for the taller *Salvia farinacea* 'Victoria,' whose vivid purple-blue spikes are in turn softened by the pale pink of penstemon hybrids.

◀ **Froth of pink** The hardy deciduous shrub *Weigela florida* 'Variegata' has delightful foliage as well as beautiful blooms. In midspring the young leaves unfold pink, white, and pale green. By midsummer they mature to dark green edged with lime-green, but before that happens, the shrub is dressed with pink-and-white flowers.

In front, the elegance of this blue *Iris pallida* 'Dalmatica' contrasts in color and form with the informality of the weigela. It is intermingled with loose sprays of the white-flowered honesty *(Lunaria annua* 'Alba').

▶ **Forget-me-not blue** *Anchusa azurea* 'Loddon Royalist' is one of the few pure blue flowers of summer. Branched flower panicles emerge from 3 ft (90 cm) stems, rising well above the coarse basal leaves. Here, in midsummer, the bare stems are hidden from view by clumps of pink and red, white-eyed sweet Williams *(Dianthus barbatus)*, which are accompanied by the yellow-green froth of lady's-mantle *(Alchemilla mollis)*.

▼ **Springtime shade** The evergreen *Bergenia* 'Ballawley' thrives in the moist soil and dappled shade of a woodland setting. Its fuchsia bell-shaped flowers match a flowering azalea and startlingly punctuate a carpet of Spanish bluebells *(Hyacinthoides hispanica)*.

▲ **Roses all the way** The little polyantha rose 'The Fairy' flowers continuously through summer and autumn, with tiny, double, clear pink blooms. In this herbaceous border it is combined with blue larkspurs (*Consolida orientalis*).

▲ **Summer contrasts** Soft cerise-pink flower clusters of *Phlox paniculata* serve as a foil for the imposing white and purple spikes of bear's-breeches (*Acanthus spinosus*). Color contrast is introduced with a planting of globe thistles (*Echinops ritro*) carrying perfect globes of steel-blue.

▶ **Splendor in spring** The graceful weeping Higan cherry (*Prunus subhirtella* 'Pendula Rubra') is ideal for the smaller garden, reaching a height of about 10 ft (3 m) at maturity, with a spread of twice that. In midspring, the wandlike branches are smothered in exquisite deep pink flowers that float above a carpet of blue *Scilla siberica*.

FORCEFUL REDS

Flowers in eye-catching reds may overwhelm in a garden, but used with discretion they can form harmonious pictures.

Red is a powerful and sometimes even aggressive color, making it tricky to handle in the garden. As a general rule, it should be used only in small doses.

Beds of all-red flowers always look best if they contain plenty of green or gray foliage plants. Make sure these foliage plants take up more room than the flowers, because too much red, even when coupled with green or gray, can be overwhelming.

If you want to combine red with other flower colors — such as blue and yellow — choose paler hues. Strong red clashes if mixed with royal blue or bright yellow.

A clever way of incorporating a full-blooded red into a mixed border is to lead the eye gently toward it, along a trail of flowers with a hint of red in them.

The siting of red also requires careful consideration. In good light, red gives the impression of moving toward the viewer. Thus, a clump of red flowers at the far end of a lawn will make a garden seem shorter — an effect you would want only if you have a long, narrow plot. In evening light, red flowers do not show up well; for patio decoration they should always be mixed with pale flower colors.

▲ **Color continuity** The dusky red velvety blooms of the Gallica rose 'Tuscany Superb' are mellowed by the sky-blue flowers of climbing morning glory (*Ipomoea tricolor*).

▼ **Pale companions** Yellow verbascums, flat-headed yarrows (*Achillea*) and pale daylilies (*Hemerocallis*) brighten a crimson and scarlet grouping of roses, dahlias, penstemons, and nicotianas.

▲ **Fire-engine red** The soft silvery-gray foliage and rambling stems of the tender *Helichrysum petiolatum* frame and subdue containers brimming with the brilliant red trumpet flowers of bedding petunias.

▶ **Snowflakes in spring** Scarlet tulip goblets glow against a backdrop of fresh green spring foliage. Their intense color is cooled by the variegated leaves and white flowers of honesty *(Lunaria annua* 'Variegata') and the delicate white bells of the summer snowflake *(Leucujum aestivum)* — which, despite its name, flowers during the spring.

◀ **Summer support** In summer the deciduous shrub *Viburnum* x *bodnantense* is dull green. Yet it is an excellent support for the vigorous *Clematis viticella* 'Royal Velour,' which weaves its stems and nodding red flowers through the dense greenery. Shading the clematis roots are clumps of blue bellflowers *(Campanula persicifolia)* and early-flowering *Allium christophii,* whose seed heads remain attractive for months. The high point for this shrub is during the winter, when it flowers abundantly.

▼ **Summer partners** The herbaceous perennials in this elegant grouping complement each other in color and form. A clump of vermilion Oriental poppies *(Papaver orientale)*, with petals like crumpled silk, flops hairy stems in front of erect spires of pink, red, and blue Russell lupines. The foliage of the poppies and lupines contrasts strongly with the bold, glossy leaves of a blue-green hosta. As summer progresses, the hosta will hide the gap left by the lupines, and the poppy flowers will be replaced by decorative seed capsules. In the background, a white-flowered clematis sheds light and airy grace over this early-summer picture.

▲ **Golden crowns** The tall stems of crown imperials *(Fritillaria imperialis* 'Aurora') are topped with clusters of drooping orange-yellow, bell-shaped flowers. They make unusual but magnificent companions for the scarlet trumpets of dwarf rhododendrons in late spring.

▶ **Study in purple**
The brilliant red evergreen azaleas at right and lower-growing rhododendrons in front are separated by a purple-leaved *Berberis thunbergii* 'Atropurpurea Nana.' In late spring a white-flowered broom *(Cytisus)* brings relief to the somber composition. During the summer the broom's wand-like green stems contrast effectively with both the leathery leaves of the rhododendron and the purple barberry.

▼ **Meadow flowers**
The blood-red *Anemone coronaria* is thought by some authorities to be the plant referred to in the biblical phrase "lilies of the field." It naturalizes easily in short grass and looks striking in the company of its smaller-flowered, pale blue relation *A. blanda.*

RED THROUGH THE YEAR

**There are shades of red to match every
season, from pale spring blossom to the red of summer
fuchsia and the purple-pink autumn crocus.**

Early spring brings pink fairy foxgloves *(Erinus alpinus)* and mossy saxifrages to the rock garden. Then cherry blossoms and pink-stained magnolia chalices burst forth, and deep pink hyacinths and scarlet tulips. Later still comes the stupendous floral display of rhododendrons and azaleas in every conceivable shade of pink and red. But the full impact of these colors belongs to the summer garden, where the tones grow steadily deeper toward true red.

There are many pink summer-flowering shrubs, such as the evergreen *Abelia × grandiflora,* with its pink and white funnels, and heavily-scented lilacs *(Syringa vulgaris)* 'Maréchal Foch'). Other varieties include the drooping clusters of pealike blooms on *Robinia hispida* and ground-hugging little rock roses, such as *Helianthemum* 'Wisley Pink,' which is massed with silky flowers the shape of single roses. The beauty bush *(Kolkwitzia amabilis)* is a fountain of porcelain-pink flowers that look like little foxgloves — they make a stunning early-summer display with a front planting of true foxgloves *(Digitalis purpurea).*

Many favorite summer flower colors are in the pink range — fuchsias with their dainty bells, peonies, astilbes, bedding pelargoniums, salvias, and petunias, and tasseled love-lies-bleeding. Roses, too, are an essential part of summer gardens. They range from splendid old shrub roses like the pale pink 'Great Maidens Blush' to the deep pink of the more recent 'Perfume Delight.'

Autumn brings fiery red leaf tints and berry clusters, pale colchicums and *Cyclamen hederifolium*, and the exotic, iridescent flower heads of *Nerine bowdenii.* Winter is brightened with plants such as red-berried hollies, daphnes, and camellias.

▼ **The essence of summer** A field of Oriental poppies *(Papaver orientale)* glows brilliant scarlet. Pink aquilegias and pale honesty *(Lunaria annua)* lend cooler tones.

▲ **Cottage-garden charm** In the bright sun of midsummer, the eye seeks the relief of soft colors. Complementary shades of pink provide such an oasis of calm, blending tall and wispy, pale pink clary *(Salvia sclarea)* with pink-flowered Canterbury bells *(Campanula medium)* and the quartered blooms of old-fashioned roses.

▲ **Bedding lobelias**
Perennial lobelias are quite different from the small blue-flowered annuals that decorate window boxes and hanging baskets in summer. The 4 ft (1.2 m) stems of *Lobelia* 'Queen Victoria' are set with purple foliage and topped with spikes of vivid red flowers. Not reliably hardy, the clumps are best overwintered in a cold frame or frost-free place and planted outside again in May.

▶ **Pink daisies** Low-growing fleabane *(Erigeron* x *hybridus)* thrives in sunny rock gardens and raised beds, opening yellow-centered, pink daisy flowers throughout summer. A close relative, *E. karvinskianus*, with tiny white or pink flowers, is invasive, seeding itself in every crack and corner.

▲ **Bowls of beauty** The peony *(Paeonia lactiflora)* has been called the queen of perennials. Though the early-summer flowering season is short, it is more than compensated for by the magnificent bowl-shaped blooms in shades of pink, red, or white. Peonies are often paired with tall bearded irises which display blue, lilac, or mauve flowers above elegant sword-shaped leaf fans.

◄ **Autumn berries** Normally a creeping shrub, this evergreen cotoneaster makes a colorful small tree when grafted onto an upright trunk. Clouds of pinkish flowers set off the lustrous green leaves in late spring, while the red berries that follow make one of fall's finest shows.

127

▲ **Autumn crocus** The slender goblets of this Agrippa autumn crocus (*Colchicum agrippinum*) open during fall to rosy lilac stars. Their bright color and naked stems demand some kind of muted foil, which is supplied here by the gray-green leaves and misty blue flower spikes of catmint (*Nepeta* x *faassenii*).

▲ **Glossy fruits** The red-tinted stems of the small evergreen shrub *Pernettya mucronata* are smothered in early summer with tiny white flowers. In fall and winter they become glistening clusters of jewellike berries ranging in color from white through pink and red to purple. For berries to be produced, male and female plants must be grown together. They prefer acid soil.

◀ **Autumn dress**
The common spindle tree (*Euonymus europaea*) is a vigorous deciduous shrub that thrives in alkaline soil. In fall, the foliage assumes soft yellow tints, but the plant's real glory lies in its huge clusters of seed capsules. In the variety 'Red Cascade' they are rose-red and so abundant they weigh down the branches.

◄ **From fall into winter** Color in the winter garden comes from evergreens — green or golden conifers — as well as from shrubs with variegated leaves, spectacular berries, or the unexpected bonus of flowers. The firethorns *(Pyracantha)* are among the most dependable berrying shrubs; the variety 'Mohave' has orange-red fruit, which birds usually leave alone. Included in this cheerful winter scene is a silver-white variegated English holly *(Ilex aquifolium)*. On the right, *Viburnum tinus* shows off flat heads of pink-budded, white flowers among glossy leaves.

▼ **Spring growth** Rivaling the shrubby pieris in splendor, the evergreen *Photinia x fraseri* is ideal for gardens with loamy, well-drained soils. Given shelter and sun, the young growths unfold in spring, becoming coppery red candles that set the leathery dark green foliage ablaze with color.

▶ **Cherry blossom** The Japanese cherry *Prunus* 'Shirofugen' is one of the final ornamental cherries to bloom, in late spring. But the flowers are worth waiting for, creating a stunning canopy from long-stalked clusters of large double flowers. Purple-pink in bud, they open white, only to turn eventually to purple-pink again. They contrast exquisitely with the coppery red young leaves. Wide-spreading and up to 30 ft (10 m) tall, the cherry casts subtle highlights over a bold woodland planting of bright red azaleas.

◀ **Spring quinces** Most familiar to Americans as a fruit and a source of jelly, the quince has been popular in the Orient for centuries as a garden shrub. The one shown here is the Chinese type, *Chaenomeles speciosa*, which may reach a height of 10 ft (3 m). It bears its pink, red, or white flowers in midspring — just as this leopard's-bane *(Doronicum plantagineum)* opens its bouquet of yellow, daisylike flowers. In front, *Euphorbia epithymoides* offers smooth domes of brilliant yellow-green foliage and flower bracts.

	PINK AND RED FLOWERS			
	NAME	**DESCRIPTION AND SITE**	**HEIGHT**	**SEASON**
TREES AND SHRUBS	*Andromeda polifolia*	Evergreen, low-growing; moist acid soil; sun	1½ ft (45 cm)	Spring
	Chaenomeles spp. and cvs.	Deciduous; fall fruit; any soil; sun	3-6 ft (90-180 cm)	Spring
	Cistus x purpureus	Evergreen, fairly hardy; well-drained soil; sun	2-6 ft (60-180 cm)	Summer
	Clethra alnifolia 'Rosea'	Deciduous; fall tints; moist acid soil; sun	6-8 ft (1.8-2.4 m)	Summer
	Cornus kousa 'Rosabella'	Deciduous; fall tints; well-drained acid soil; sun	25 ft (7.5 m)	Early summer
	Crataegus laevigata cvs.	Deciduous trees; fall fruit; any soil; sun	18-25 ft (5.4-7.5 m)	Spring
	Daphne x burkwoodii	Semievergreen; well-drained soil; sun or light shade	3-4 ft (90-120 cm)	Spring–early summer
	Daphne cneorum	Evergreen; well-drained soil; sun or light shade	1 ft (30 cm)	Spring–early summer
	Daphne mezereum	Deciduous; upright; well-drained soil; sun	5 ft (1.5 m)	Spring
	Deutzia scabra	Deciduous; well-drained soil; sun	8 ft (2.4 m)	Late spring–summer
	Eccremocarpus scaber	Evergreen, near-hardy climber; rich, moist soil; sun, sheltered wall	8-10 ft (2.4-3 m)	Summer–fall
	Escallonia hybrids	Evergreen, best in seaside gardens; well-drained soil; sun	5-8 ft (1.5-2.4 m)	Spring–fall
	Helianthemum nummularium cvs.	Evergreen, wide-spreading; well-drained soil; sun	1-2 ft (30-60 cm)	Summer
	Hibiscus syriacus cvs.	Deciduous; hardy; well-drained soil; sun	8-12 ft (2.4-3.6 m)	Summer–fall
	Indigofera spp.	Deciduous; near-hardy; rich soil; sun; shelter	4 ft (1.2 m)	Summer–fall
	Kalmia latifolia	Evergreen; moist acid soil; sun or shade	6-15 ft (1.8-4.5 m)	Summer
	Kolkwitzia amabilis	Deciduous; thicket forming; any soil; sun	6-12 ft (1.8-3.6 m)	Summer
	Leycesteria formosa	Deciduous; near-hardy; any soil; sun or shade	6 ft (1.8 m)	Summer
	Lonicera x heckrottii	Deciduous climber; well-drained soil; sun or shade	10-20 ft (3-6 m)	Summer–fall
	Lonicera sempervirens	Semievergreen climber; loamy soil; sun or shade	10-20 ft (3-6 m)	Summer
	Magnolia x loebneri 'Leonard Messel'	Deciduous; moist, well-drained soil; sun	15 ft (4.5 m)	Early spring
	Magnolia x soulangiana cvs.	Deciduous; well-drained soil; sun	20-30 ft (6-9 m)	Spring
	Malus floribunda	Deciduous; fall fruit; any soil; sun	15 ft (4.5 m)	Spring
	Paeonia suffruticosa hybrids	Deciduous; handsome foliage; well-drained neutral soil; sun; shelter	4 ft (1.2 m)	Early summer
	Potentilla fruticosa cvs.	Deciduous; compact; well-drained soil; sun	1-4 ft (30-120 cm)	Early summer–fall
	Prunus spp. and cvs.	Deciduous shrubs and trees; well-drained soil; sun	2-20 ft (60-600 cm)	Spring
	Ribes sanguineum	Deciduous; well-drained soil; sun or shade	6-8 ft (1.8-2.4 m)	Spring
	Robinia hispida	Deciduous; well-drained soil; sun; shelter	6 ft (1.8 m)	Late spring
	Spiraea x bumalda	Deciduous; wide-spreading; rich soil; sun	2½-3 ft (75-90 cm)	Summer
	Tamarix ramosissima	Deciduous; feathery foliage; best in seaside garden; well-drained soil; sun	10-15 ft (3-4.5 m)	Summer
	Tropaeolum speciosum	Deciduous near-hardy climber; any well-drained soil; sun	15 ft (4.5 m)	Summer–early fall
	Viburnum x bodnantense	Deciduous; moist, well-drained soil; sun	9-12 ft (2.7-3.6 m)	Winter
	Weigela spp. and cvs.	Deciduous; well-drained soil; sun or light shade	5-6 ft (1.5-1.8 m)	Summer
ANNUALS	*Agrostemma githago*	Hardy, self-seeding; well-drained soil; sun	2-3 ft (60-90 cm)	Summer
	Amaranthus tricolor	Half-hardy; colorful leaves; any soil; sun	4 ft (1.2 m)	Late summer–fall
	Callistephus chinensis	Half-hardy, good as cut flowers; any soil; sun	½-2½ ft (15-75 cm)	Summer–fall
	Centaurea cyanus cvs.	Hardy and easy; well-drained soil; sun	1½-3 ft (45-90 cm)	Summer–fall
	Clarkia unguilculata	Hardy, double-flowered; well-drained soil; sun	1-2 ft (30-60 cm)	Summer–fall
	Clarkia rubicunda	Hardy, bushy; well-drained soil; sun	9-20 in (23-50 cm)	Summer
	Cleome hasslerana	Half-hardy, well-drained soil; sun	3-6 ft (90-180 cm)	Summer–fall
	Cosmos bipinnatus	Half-hardy, ferny leaves; well-drained soil; sun	2-5 ft (60-150 cm)	Summer–fall
	Gomphrena globosa cvs.	Half-hardy, suitable for drying; any soil; sun	½-2½ ft (15-75 cm)	Summer–fall
	Helichrysum bracteatum cvs.	Half-hardy; suitable for drying; any soil; sun	1-3 ft (30-90 cm)	Summer–early fall
	Iberis umbellata	Hardy; easy, good for cutting; any soil; sun	1 ft (30 cm)	Summer–fall
	Linaria maroccana	Hardy; any soil; sun	8-12 in (20-30 cm)	Summer

NAME	DESCRIPTION AND SITE	HEIGHT	SEASON
ANNUALS (cont.)			
Linum grandiflorum	Hardy, easy; well-drained soil; sun	1-1½ ft (30-45 cm)	Summer
Malcolmia maritima	Hardy, fragrant; well-drained soil; sun	½-1 ft (15-30 cm)	Spring–fall
Matthiola incana cvs.	Hardy, richly scented; good soil; sun or light shade	1-2½ ft (30-75 cm)	Summer
Mimulus hybrids	Half-hardy, compact; moist soil; shade	½-1 ft (15-30 cm)	Spring–fall
Papaver nudicaule	Hardy, large blooms; any soil; sun	15-18 in (40-45 cm)	Late spring
Papaver rhoeas	Hardy, seedpods; any, even poor soil; sun	2-3 ft (60-90 cm)	Summer
Salvia splendens	Half-hardy, bedding plants; well-drained soil; sun	1-3 ft (30-90 cm)	Summer–fall
Schizanthus pinnatus 'Roseus'	Half-hardy, fernlike foliage; moist soil; sun; shelter	4 ft (1.2 m)	Summer–fall
PERENNIALS, BULBS, CORMS, AND TUBERS			
Aethionema x warleyense	Evergreen subshrub; well-drained alkaline soil; sun	6-9 in (15-23 cm)	Late spring–summer
Allium roseum	Bulbous, long-lasting; well-drained soil; sun	1 ft (30 cm)	Early summer
Amaryllis belladonna	Half-hardy bulb; sandy loam; sun; shelter	1½ ft (45 cm)	Fall
Anemone x hybrida cvs.	Tough once established; moist soil; sun or shade	2½-5 ft (75-150 cm)	Late summer–fall
Armeria maritima	Evergreen, clump forming; well-drained soil; sun	1 ft (30 cm)	Spring–summer
Astilbe spp. and cvs.	Attractive foliage; moist to wet soil; sun or shade	1½-4 ft (45-120 cm)	Summer
Bergenia spp. and cvs.	Evergreen, leathery leaves; any soil; sun or shade	1-2 ft (30-60 cm)	Early–late spring
Centaurea dealbata	Deeply cut, hairy leaves; well-drained soil; sun	2 ft (60 cm)	Early summer–fall
Centranthus ruber	Extremely hardy; well-drained soil; sun	1½-3 ft (45-90 cm)	Summer
Chrysanthemum coccineum	Feathery foliage; light soil; sun	2½-3 ft (75-90 cm)	Late spring–early fall
Dicentra eximia	Delicately cut foliage; rich, moist, well-drained soil; some shade	1½ ft (45 cm)	Summer
Dierama pulcherrimum	Grassy foliage; well-drained rich soil; sun; shelter	3-6 ft (90-180 cm)	Late summer–fall
Digitalis x mertonensis	Evergreen, tapering spikes; moist soil; light shade	2-3 ft (60-90 cm)	Late spring–summer
Echinacea purpurea	Sturdy, tough, long bloom period; any soil; sun	2-5 ft (60-150 cm)	Summer
Erythronium dens-canis	Brown-blotched leaves; rich, moist soil; shade	4-6 in (10-15 cm)	Spring
Eupatorium purpureum	Suitable for semiwild areas; moist soil; sun or shade	4-6 ft (1.2-1.8 m)	Summer–fall
Euphorbia griffithii 'Fireglow'	Herbaceous, colorful bracts; any soil; sun	2-3 ft (60-90 cm)	Late spring
Filipendula purpurea	Hand-shaped foliage; any soil; sun or light shade	1-4 ft (30-120 cm)	Late summer–fall
Geum quellyon cvs.	Clump forming; well-drained soil; sun or light shade	1-2 ft (30-60 cm)	Summer
Helleborus orientalis	Handsome, near-evergreen foliage; deep, moist soil; shade	2 ft (60 cm)	Winter–spring
Heuchera sanguinea	Hairy leaf mats; light soil; sun or light shade	2 ft (60 cm)	Spring–summer
Incarvillea delavayi	Handsome lobed leaves; moist, well-drained soil; sun	2 ft (60 cm)	Spring–early summer
Kniphofia cvs.	Specimen plants; rich, well-drained soil; sun	2-4 ft (60-120 cm)	Summer–fall
Lamium maculatum cvs.	Excellent ground cover; any soil; sun or shade	1 ft (30 cm)	Spring–fall
Liatris spicata	Grassy leaf clumps; well-drained soil; sun	3 ft (90 cm)	Late summer
Lobelia spp. and cvs.	Handsome foliage; rich, moist soil; light shade	2½-4 ft (75-120 cm)	Summer–fall
Lychnis spp.	Often silvery foliage; any soil; sun	1-3 ft (30-90 cm)	Late spring–summer
Malva alcea	Hardy; any soil; sun or light shade	2-4 ft (60-120 cm)	Summer–fall
Nerine bowdenii	Bulbous, half-hardy; well-drained soil; sun; wall shelter	15 in (40 cm)	Fall
Paeonia lactiflora cvs.	Long-lived, handsome foliage; rich well-drained soil; sun or light shade	2-3 ft (60-90 cm)	Early summer
Papaver orientale cvs.	Hardy, floppy habit, hairy; well-drained soil; sun	2-3 ft (60-90 cm)	Early summer
Penstemon spp. and cvs.	Border and rock plants; well-drained soil; sun	4-36 in (10-90 cm)	Spring–summer
Phlox paniculata cvs.	Long-lived; fertile soil; sun	to 40 in (1 m)	Summer–fall
Physostegia virginiana	Hardy, trouble free; moist soil; sun or shade	3 ft (90 cm)	Summer–fall
Saponaria ocymoides	Vigorous and compact; well-drained soil; sun or light shade	6 in (15 cm)	Late spring–summer
Schizostylis coccinea	Near-hardy bulb; moist soil; sun; shelter	2-3 ft (60-90 cm)	Fall
Stokesia laevis	Easy, hardy; light, well-drained soil; sun	1-1½ ft (30-45 cm)	Summer–fall
Thymus spp. and cvs.	Evergreen creeping mats; well-drained soil; sun	½-1 ft (15-30 cm)	Summer
Zauschneria californica	Near-hardy, grassy foliage; light, well-drained soil; sun; shelter	1-3 ft (30-90 cm)	Summer–fall

Blue and mauve flowers

Echoing the color of the sky, blue flowers come in many shades. They range from the cool, crisp colors of a spring morning to the misty gray-blues of autumn, and from the near-purple of gathering dusk to rich midnight blue. Some popular border plants, such as irises and delphiniums, are available in all these variations, while others have such distinctive tones that they have become part of our descriptive language; think of forget-me-not and cornflower blue.

There are few pure blue flowers. The majority incline either to cool white-blue shades or dark and intense purples and violet-reds. And in spite of many attempts and much cross-breeding, there are no truly blue roses or tulips although the hybrid tea rose 'Blue Skies' or the 'Blue Parrot' tulip can be successfully incorporated in all-blue plantings. Luckily, blue flowers rarely clash with one another. Some of the most beautiful, however, like the gentians and the Himalayan blue poppies (*Meconopsis* species), have exacting growing demands that exclude them from many soils and sites.

Clear blues — campanulas and agapanthus, for example — look cool and tranquil. Like pale blue, they are most effective in dark settings. Picture bluebells in dappled woodland light or *Rhododendron augustinii* against its own glossy dark green foliage. Dark blues have little impact from a distance, although they can be exquisite up close or in pale surroundings. Rich blue monkshoods *(Aconitum)* contrast magnificently with golden-leaved spiraeas or elder *(Sambucus racemosa* 'Plumosa Aurea'). Violet and purple shades — in asters, lilacs, violas, and pansies — can introduce warmth and contrast to potentially sugary pale blues.

True blue 'Pacific Hybrid' delphiniums offer the full range of blues, from sky to ink.

COOL AND DISTANT BLUES

**Groupings of all-blue flowers create
a cool, relaxing atmosphere and can make
a small garden appear larger.**

Blue flowers range from cold, even frosty tints to deeper, warmer, more purple shades that carry a hint of red. Such variety means that blues mix well with most other colors — and they also form successful groupings by themselves. In a monochromatic design the range of blue shades and tints creates interest, yet because the flowers are essentially the same color, the grouping is harmonious.

When creating blue combinations, keep in mind the following points. Light blues, surrounded by gray or silver foliage, become more luminous, making them excellent choices for beds around a patio where you sit or entertain in the evening. Blues with a touch of red will be less luminous, but they can be used to add warmth to groupings dominated by cool blues.

All blues, but especially the paler tints, recede — they draw the eye after them. This quality makes them invaluable for giving the impression of extra depth. Placed at the end of a small plot, the misty blues of forget-me-nots, catmint, delphiniums, caryopteris, and some of the Michaelmas daisies can make such a garden look longer than it really is.

The use of a single color means that the form, texture, and overall growth pattern of the plants should be considered carefully to avoid monotony. In spring, a successful grouping of blue-flowered bulbs might include the spiked flower heads of grape hyacinths *(Muscari armeniacum)*, the delicate star-shaped *Chionodoxa*, and blue forms of the daisylike *Anemone blanda*.

In a sunny herbaceous border in summer, good contrast is provided by planting the pincushion-like flower heads of *Scabiosa caucasica* alongside *Linum narbonense* (which has sparkling funnels for blooms). Then add the saucer-shaped flowers of *Veronica*

▶ **Partners for a rose**
In early summer the shrub rose 'Nevada' becomes a fountain of gorgeous blooms, whose white crispness is complemented by spires of blue delphiniums and the delicate bells of *Campanula persicifolia*. In the foreground a clump of spiderwort *(Tradescantia × andersoniana)* continues the blue theme to ground level.

135

▲ Rock garden in spring A lightly shaded rock garden is the ideal site for the little squill *(Scilla siberica)*. Violet cress *(Ionopsidium acaule)* is a good companion; this diminutive annual, only 2 in (5 cm) high, can be sown in fall. It will bloom into a close, lilac-tinted carpet the following spring.

▲ Harmony in lilac Irises and lupines make perfect partners in an all-blue arrangement in a summer border. The pale lilac-blue blooms of this bearded iris lend emphasis to the contrasting elegant spikes of darker Russell lupines. Additional contrast is found in the foliage, where the stiff blue-green sword-shaped leaves of the iris serve to support the floppy sage-green lupine foliage.

◄ Carpet of blue The sweetly scented evergreen *Daphne odora* 'Aureomarginata' has a somewhat sprawling growth pattern. Its appearance is improved with a carpet of blue spring flowers. Try dark blue *Viola labradorica* 'Purple Leaf' with the clear daisylike flowers of *Anemone blanda*, the club-shaped heads of pale blue *Muscari armeniacum* and, in back, a cloud of Spanish bluebells *(Hyacinthoides hispanicus)*.

▲ **Clothing a wall in color** This outstanding grouping is eye-catching for its imaginative use of contrasting flower shapes and shades. The deciduous ceanothus blooms for most of the summer in the shelter of the sunny wall. It is laden with fluffy panicles of misty blue that offset the nodding sky-blue flowers of the climbing *Clematis* 'Perle d'Azur.'

Below, reveling in the warmth of the site, a clump of agapanthus raises huge, rounded heads of violet-blue flowers.

► **Texas's pride** The official flower of the Lone Star State, bluebonnets *(Lupinus texensis)* flood fields and roadsides there with sapphire blue in springtime. Equally beautiful in the garden, these hardy annuals may be started in the South from seed sown outdoors in early fall, and in the North in pots kept indoors in late winter.

▲ Frosty-white blues The spring-flowering *Puschkinia scilloides* is also called striped squill for the icy blue stripes on its white hyacinthlike clusters. It blends well with the purple foliage and flowers of the pansy *Viola labradorica* 'Purple Leaf.'

▶ Purple warmth Purple-blue spikes of *Salvia × superba* introduce a hint of warmth to tall, cool blue delphiniums.

▼ Summer cool Pale blue campanulas and white-eyed delphiniums mixed with white lavateras create a pool of refreshing calm in the heat of summer.

BLUE AND YELLOW

Groupings of complementary blues and yellows give character and a sense of individuality to the smallest garden.

Blue is a popular color with many gardeners, but the paler tones can appear frosty and hard unless they are enlivened with touches of warmer colors. Also, the warm shades of violet and mauve can appear dull and lost in their own shadows unless brighter flowers enclose them. In both instances, yellow flowers are the perfect companions, warming cool blue tints and bringing dark shades into sharp relief.

Color harmony is a basic element in good garden design, but successful combinations are not achieved by simply mixing two color ranges. Harmony — or contrast — in shape and texture is just as important. Avoid mixing too many daisy flowers or spikes or fluffy panicles. Instead, include contrasting shapes, such as slender spires of lavender-blue catmint *(Nepeta × faassenii)* with the yellow or orange daisy flowers of pot marigolds *(Calendula officinalis)*. Or try pale blue, club-shaped grape hyacinths *(Muscari armeniacum)* against the pale yellow *Primula vulgaris*.

Spring and summer partners
Blue and yellow are natural spring partners. Pair forget-me-nots with pale yellow tulips or golden-orange wallflowers, or porcelain-blue chionodoxas with yellow *Aurinia saxatilis*. By the pool, place slender blue Jacob's ladder *(Polemonium caeruleum)* above the glistening gold of double-flowered marsh marigolds *(Caltha palustris* 'Flore Pleno').

In summer, cool mixtures of blue and yellow can be calming amidst more vibrant colors. Blue irises or delphiniums can be paired with yellow shrub roses. Formal beds of the hybrid tea rose 'Oregold' appear even more luminous within a front edge of clear blue *Geranium* 'Johnson's Blue.' The pale blue *Clematis* 'Mrs Cholmondeley' looks magnificent against a wall when accompanied by the yellow climbing rose 'Mermaid.' Impressive focal points can be created in the herbaceous border with clumps of sky-blue Himalayan poppies *(Meconopsis betonicifolia)* rising up from a footing of golden-leaved *Hosta fortunei* 'Albopicta.'

Although blue is scarce in autumn, Michaelmas daisies and the blue flowers of *Aster novi-belgii* 'Professor Kippenburg' can be set against deep yellow *Kniphofia* 'Gold Mine.'

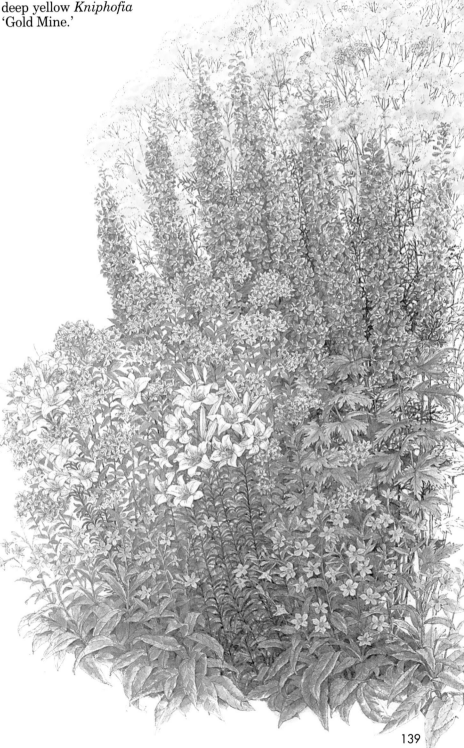

▼ **Peaceful scene** Placed before yellow meadow rue *(Thalictrum speciosissimum)*, delphiniums and bellflowers create an oasis of calm in summertime with madonna lilies *(Lilium candidum)* and *Nicotiana alata* 'Lime Green.'

▶ **Asters to the fore** Amellus asters can be a better choice than the related Michaelmas daisies, since they are both long-lived and trouble-free. A hybrid from that species, *Aster x frikartii,* fills the late-summer border with daisy-flowered blooms for several months. Lavender-blue in the variety 'Moench,' it is shadowed here by the towering 4 ft (1.2 m) stems of *Oenothera erythrosepala,* set with golden-yellow flower funnels.

▼ **Heavenly blue** From early summer until early fall, the prostrate alpine *Lithodora diffusa* 'Heavenly Blue' spreads a shrubby mat over the rock garden, although here it is almost hidden by a profusion of deep blue funnel-shaped flowers. The flowers are beautifully set off by the golden-yellow clusters of *Genista lydia* and the young gold-tipped shoots of a dwarf spruce *(Abies).* In the foreground a shield fern *(Dryopteris)* raises its sage-green fronds in the sea of blue.

▶ **Summer beds** The hardy annual *Ipomoea tricolor* has all of the advantages and none of the difficulties associated with its close relative, bindweed. The variety 'Blue Ensign' forms compact plants, about 5 in (15 cm) high, with brilliant blue flowers whose centers are marked with white-and-yellow stars. It blooms from summer until early fall. Here it is grouped effectively with floppy, golden-yellow California poppies *(Eschscholzia californica)* guarded by tall-stemmed, white-flowered penstemon hybrids.

◀ **Winter joy** Undamaged by snow and frost, the small bulbous *Iris histrioides* 'Major' sends up its royal blue flowers in midwinter. It is distinguished by a narrow orange ridge on the lower falls of the blooms, echoed in the orange stamens of the February-flowering *Crocus chrysanthus*. Both plants thrive in light, dappled shade but show off their intense colors best in full sun.

▲ **Blue-and-yellow duet** The satiny blue flowers of *Geranium ibericum*, with mounds of deeply lobed leaves, nestle at the base of 3 ft (90 cm) tall *Phlomis russeliana*, set with tiers of creamy yellow tubular flowers.

▼ **Easter joy** The little pasqueflower (*Anemone pulsatilla*) opens its downy buds to purple, golden-centered cups in late spring. At the same time the 6 in (15 cm) high *Tulipa tarda* spreads its yellow petals into wide stars.

▲ **Summer tapestry** *Salvia patens*, a half-hardy annual, weaves its clear blue flowers through equally tender primrose-yellow *Argyranthemum frutescens*. The daisy-flower shape is repeated in the golden gazanias.

BLUE AND ORANGE

Create eye-catching groups with clusters of blue flowers that complement and soften vivid orange flowers.

Complementary colors enliven one another, and few combinations are as powerful as blue and orange. Use these bold mixtures carefully to create arrangements providing welcome contrast to the more subtle colors that usually dominate the garden.

The brilliance of such contrasts can be toned down by using a lighter tint of one color with a darker shade of the other. In spring, pale forget-me-nots make a misty blue carpet for startling orange tulips, such as 'Orange Bouquet,' or orange wallflowers, such as 'Allegretto.' This group could be planted at the front of a mixed border and later replaced by summer bedding. For an enchanting display using a similar color theme, grow the petunia 'Resisto Blue' with the hot-orange French marigold 'Paprika.'

Blue and orange combinations look especially effective when chosen to contrast different growth patterns. The dense 10 in (25 cm) tufts of the graceful blue-gray perennial grass *Festuca ovina glauca* look handsome in front of the shrubby potentilla 'Tangerine,' whose coppery orange flowers appear continuously from early summer to early fall.

You might edge a bed with the little tufted pansy (*Viola cornuta* 'Blue Perfection'), whose medium blue flowers look glorious below the Welsh poppy (*Meconopsis cambrica*). Flowering the whole summer and well into fall, this poppy grows to a height of about 1½ ft (45 cm). Though usually yellow, it may also be orange.

On a sunny wall, the saucer-shaped blooms of blue morning glory (*Ipomoea tricolor*) can be strikingly combined with the orange of the Chilean glory flower (*Eccremocarpus scaber*).

▶ **Striking contrasts** The large purplish-blue flowers of *Clematis* 'Lasurstern' stand out against slender clusters of orange-yellow honeysuckle *(Lonicera* x *tellmanniana)* smothering a wall in early summer.

▶ **Good companions**
The impressive bulbous plant *Camassia leichtlinii* raises 3 ft (90 cm) tall spikes of starry flowers above tufts of grassy foliage in early summer. Their pale blue tones temper the vivid orange of a front planting of Siberian wallflowers *(Erysimum hieraciifolium).*

▲ **Late-summer brilliance** Planted in a sunny, sheltered spot, *Agapanthus* 'Headbourne Hybrids' put on a massed display of vivid blue in late summer. The rounded flower heads contrast effectively with the taller spikes of orange-red *Curtonus paniculatus*, a South African perennial.

◀ **Streaks of blue** Spikes of pale blue delphiniums add vertical interest and soften the colorful impact of a dense planting of globeflowers. Happiest in moist soil, the hybrid globeflower *(Trollius)* unfolds its brilliant orange-yellow blooms in late spring and early summer.

▶ **Unforgettably blue** Blooming from late spring through fall, forget-me-nots *(Myosotis scorpioids)* form a flood of blue. This carefree perennial (hardy to zone 5) shows even bluer set against azaleas whose scarlet blooms are tinted with orange.

▲ **A gift from the hills** The intense blue flowers of hound's tongue *(Cynoglossum nervosum)* resemble forget-me-nots, although they are borne on much taller, hairy-leaved plants that originate in the Himalayas. Flowering in midsummer, hound's tongue goes well with the arching orange-red flower spikes of *Crocosmia x crocosmiiflora.*

◄ **Summer splendor** The purple-blue flowers of the shrubby *Salvia officinalis* 'Purpurascens' lose their dominance in the company of the fragrant modern shrub rose 'Graham Thomas,' whose apricot-yellow buds open to clear yellow.

▼ **Spring bedding** The blue faces of pansies and red-gold goblets of the tulips offer a bold, complementary contrast that intensifies each flower's hue, creating a scintillating mid-spring bed.

BLUE AND RED

Create vivid color splashes in herbaceous borders and temper their impact with silvery and gray foliage plants.

Strong blues and vivid reds make for powerful, even aggressive pairings. Such groupings should always be used with discretion and in small doses, rather like exclamation marks in borders otherwise dominated by pastel colors.

Blue and red combinations are most common in the summer garden, although there are some classic late-spring groupings, such as Spanish bluebells *(Hyacinthoides hispanica)* next to red polyanthus primroses and carpets of forget-me-nots or grape hyacinths *(Muscari armeniacum)* with red or pink tulips.

Traditionally, roses of all types and colors are mixed with blue delphiniums, lavender, pansies, or catmint *(Nepeta × faassenii)*. Many climbing red roses share wall space with large-flowered blue Jackmanii clematises.

In general, it is advisable to mix strong blue flowers with deep pink and clear cerise rather than bright scarlet. Alternatively, use misty blue or lavender tones to partner crimson and purple-red shades. It is, however, possible to position two strong colors near each other as long as they are separated by foliage plants that harmonize with both. Silvery plants such as *Stachys byzantina*, wormwood *(Artemisia absinthium)*, and *Senecio cineraria* 'Silverdust' are particularly effective as foils among brilliantly colored blooms.

Tender bedding fuchsias are so exquisite in bloom that they demand companions that complement rather than compete with their beauty. You might underplant container-grown fuchsias like the red and purple 'Papoose' with pale blue annual *Lobelia erinus* 'Cambridge Blue.' Or edge a mixed border with the clear blue cups of *Campanula carpatica*.

The lavender-blue bells of *Campanula lactiflora* are indispensable in any summer border; they look magnificent with almost any other combination of flowers and in particular with the spires of penstemons. Try placing the bellflowers next to varieties of *Penstemon campanulatus,* such as the scarlet 'Firebird' or the rose-pink 'Evelyn.'

Against a sheltered and sunny wall that is dressed with a blue passionflower vine *(Passiflora caerulea)* — which blooms from June until fall — a footing of clear pink petunias makes a perfect companion.

◄ **Autumn brilliance** The silver-white woolly foliage of *Artemisia ludoviciana* separates two vivid colors in this early-fall scene. At the back are the bright pink daisy flowers of *Aster novae-angliae* 'Harrington's Pink,' whose color is complemented by the carmine flower domes of *Sedum spectabile* 'Carmen' in front. Effective contrast in color and form is provided by the agapanthus, whose bright blue flower umbels rise above clumps of glossy green leaves.

▲ **Spring carpets** Grape hyacinths
(Muscari armeniacum) spread readily to
form a carpet of cobalt-blue, punctuated
by the perfect reddish-purple globes of the
drumstick primrose *(Primula denticulata).*

▶ **Summer brightness** Violet *Geranium
ibericum* will remain in bloom long
after these peonies have enjoyed their
brilliant but brief display.

▼ **Rose companions** Catmint
(Nepeta x *faassenii)* flowers through
summer and fall. It is an ideal edging
plant for roses. Here it fronts the clear
pink shrub rose 'Constance Spry.'

WARM AND COOL PURPLES

For pretty plant groupings use the subtle range of purples to bridge the gap between tints of blue, violet, and pinkish red.

Purple can be one of the gentler colors in the garden. Its soft and misty shades range from pinkish blue to the paler shades of violet. Choose from the wide range of purple flowers to complement pink, pinkish-blue, and violet-flowering plants, and perhaps to combine with gray- and silver-toned foliage.

Such harmonious combinations look elegant in window boxes or in containers on a porch, patio, or deck. For long-lasting effect, complement purple, pink, and blue petunias with the silvery leaves of *Senecio cineraria.*

For color contrast with purple, especially its deeper, bluer shades, choose pale yellow flowers, such as the yellowish greens of foaming lady's-mantle *(Alchemilla mollis)* or *Angelica archangelica* with its rounded flower heads.

In middle and late spring, sulfur-yellow *Aurinia saxatilis* 'Citrinum' is a good partner for purple aubrietas. Unlike the bright yellow of its normal form, this cultivar creates a calm pairing for rock gardens and retaining walls.

Several rhododendrons have purple flowers, including the popular *Rhododendron ponticum* — a useful evergreen screen. A combination that has long-lasting interest is evergreen *Helleborus lividus corsicus* with *Corydalis lutea* in the foreground. The hellebore's cup-shaped, apple-green flowers open from early spring, before those of the rhododendron, but they remain beautiful for a long time. The corydalis produces a mass of tubular yellow flowers that last from midspring until fall.

The small hooded flowers of catmint *(Nepeta × faassenii),* in a misty shade of violet with more than a touch of blue, are set off to perfection by its gray-green foliage. From early to middle summer they look charming with *Erigeron × hybridus,* whose many-petaled daisylike blooms provide a contrasting flower form in harmonizing shades of pink and purplish pink. For a quiet background, try the finely divided gray leaves of the 3 ft (90 cm) tall wormwood *(Artemisia absinthium* 'Lambrook Silver'). Alternatively, for a contrast in color and flower form, plant a clump of pale yellow daylilies with large, upward-facing trumpet-shaped flowers. At the rear, imposing delphiniums in purples and pinks might add vertical interest.

Acanthus spinosus — bear's-breech — carries its purple and white hooded flowers in middle and late summer on long-lasting statuesque spikes that are up to 5 ft (1.5 m) tall. The beautiful, deeply divided leaves are best grouped with plants that have contrasting foliage forms but flowers that harmonize with the acanthus. A suitable foreground partner, for example, is the 2 ft (60 cm) tall *Sedum maximum* 'Atropurpureum,' with similarly colored flower heads and purple, rather rounded and fleshy leaves. Alongside the acanthus, plant *Aster × frikartii* 'Moench,' with soft lavender-blue, yellow-centered daisies that last until early fall. Behind, to complete the group, try the tree mallow *(Lavatera olbia),* which bears its purple-pink, hollyhocklike flowers until the arrival of the early frosts.

◄ **Shades of purple** The stately foxglove *(Digitalis purpurea)* makes a stunning impression in summer with its tall spikes rising above hairy leaves. The 'Excelsior' strain includes white, pink, and purple flowers, worthy companions for the dark *Rosa rugosa* 'Roseraie de l'Hay.' The color theme is strengthened by a front planting of magenta *Geranium psilostemon* and frothy pink bells of *Heuchera × brizoides* 'Scintillation.'

◀ **Elegant purples** The Californian annual *Clarkia unguiculata* covers a wide color range, from pink and scarlet or orange and white to lavender and purple. It blooms nonstop from midsummer until early fall. Here its colorful, 1½-ft (45-cm) tall spikes of flowers draw the eye upward from the foliage of two companions that have finished flowering, irises and Oriental poppies.

▼ **Summer pastels** The clear mauve lacy caps of *Hydrangea aspera aspera* are in perfect harmony with the crisp pink clusters of *Phlox paniculata*. A background of the purple-leaved *Berberis thunbergii* 'Rosy Glow' perfectly highlights the pastel colors in front.

▲ **Winter tapestry** The evergreen heath *(Erica carnea)* is a popular winter-flowering plant. It forms wide mounds of attractive ground cover and from late fall until well into spring blossoms with neat sprays of white, pink, red, and true purple flowers.

Here, the deep pinkish-purple 'Winter Beauty' is pierced in spring by the dainty stems and glossy straplike leaves of the aptly named glory-of-the-snow *(Chionodoxa luciliae)*. Its porcelain-blue, white-centered flowers gleam like jewels among the flowers and leaves of the heather.

▼ **Summer abundance** A bold blend of pale and deeper mauve erupts in sheer exuberance on this garden wall in early summer. Two clematis hybrids entwine, giving each other support. Neither overpowers the other, so they create a picture of perfect harmony.

In the foreground the delicate sprays of meadow rue *(Thalictrum delavayi)* repeat the color theme, while its ferny foliage adds a delicate footnote. On a practical level, the foliage also provides the necessary shade over the shallow clematis roots, which must be protected from strong sun.

◀ **Color in the shade** The Lenten rose *(Helleborus orientalis)* first opens its nodding flower cups in late winter and goes on well into spring. Extremely variable in color, the flowers may be cream or white, pink, or plum-colored, but they are always heavily flecked with crimson-purple inside, as if to show off the golden-yellow stamens. Shade-loving Lenten roses are ideal for the front of shrub borders, accompanied in early spring by small pink-flowered *Primula vulgaris*. After flowering, they suppress weeds with their leathery evergreen leaves.

▼ **Unfolding blazes** With its grassy foliage and dense flower spikes, blazing star, or gayfeather *(Liatris spicata)*, resembles a small red-hot poker. Unlike the latter, though, liatris opens its flowers from the top down, until the spike is a living flame of vibrant color in the late-summer bed. Against this dramatic purple-pink background a stand of clear pink snapdragons appears almost translucent.

BLUE THROUGH THE YEAR

**Cool blues and rich purples follow the
progress of the seasons, echoing the changing
sky and the intensity of daylight.**

Blue is the color of many cheerful bulbs that greet the spring — purple-blue crocuses and clear blue muscaris, scillas, and hyacinths. They are joined by the pretty cup-shaped *Anemone apennina* and *A. blanda* and, in shady rock gardens, by *Hepatica nobilis,* which is often mistaken for an anemone.

There are purple-blue rhododendrons *(R. augustinii* and *R. ponticum)* and the magnificent Kurume azaleas. One broom, *Cytisus* 'Lilac Time,' departs from the usual yellow flowers of the species to wreathe its wandlike stems in purple pealike blooms in late spring.

Most blue flowers, though, belong in the summer garden.

Few borders are without such ever-popular plants as delphiniums, bellflowers, irises, sweet peas, lupines, and scabiosas. The vivid blue gentians can be difficult to grow, but they are exquisite in form and color. The spring-flowering *Gentiana acaulis* is less difficult than the starlike *G. verna,* which demands alkaline soil to thrive. *G. septemfida,* which in spite of its name flowers in middle and late summer, is the easiest of all to grow, bearing clusters of deep blue trumpetlike flowers.

From zone 8 southward the ceanothuses — evergreen and deciduous — continue to offer a lavish assortment of blues into fall. Far hardier (to zone 5) is

Buddleia davidii, beloved by butterflies. The cultivar 'Black Knight' bears deep purple flowers; purple-blue is also the color of *Clematis heracleifolia.* This is not the usual climbing clematis but a true herbaceous perennial, which in early autumn bears tubular flowers on stems 3 ft (90 cm) tall.

Winter blues in the garden are possible from zone 8 southward with the use of pansies and the brilliant blue little *Iris histrioides* and *I. reticulata.*

▼ **Perennial blues** Large-flowered delphinium hybrids come in all shades of blue, clearer and brighter than the nearby sprays of *Anchusa azurea.* Pink lupines complete the picture.

▶ **Summer exotics** At the height of summer, the graceful umbels of violet-blue *Agapanthus* 'Headbourne Hybrids' unfold above clumps of narrow strap-shaped leaves. They contrast in shape with the slender stems of exotic-looking Cape fuchsia *(Phygelius capensis)*, tinkling with scarlet tubular flowers, and with the deeply cut foliage of the tree peony *(Paeonia lutea ludlowii)* in the background.

▼ **Shades of purple** In this semiwild setting, pale purple Jackmanii clematis scrambles through the branching stems of pale magenta wood betony *(Stachys grandiflora)* in the foreground. In rear stand brooding dark blue spikes of delphiniums — the Blackmore and Langdon strain of this perennial favorite offers a mix of colors and magnificent flower bloom.

▲ **Summer clouds** Airy lilac wands of catmint *(Nepeta x faassenii)* are a perfect foil for the pale yellow trumpets of fleeting daylilies *(Hemerocallis* hybrids). Both are hardy border perennials that increase steadily over the years. Catmint flowers throughout summer and fall, long after the daylilies have died back to grassy clumps of foliage.

◄ **Autumn blues** In late summer and early fall, Russian sage *(Perovskia atriplicifolia)* decks its downy gray-white stems with a mass of small violet-blue flowers. Their tubular shape is repeated in the clear pink spikes of the hybrid penstemons.

► **Autumn fruits** The evergreen shrub *Berberis darwinii*, named in honor of Charles Darwin, is a year-long delight. In spring the glossy leaves are hidden behind showers of brilliant orange-yellow blooms. By fall the branches are weighed down with clusters of blue-black grape-bloomed fruit. At a height and spread of 8 ft (2.4 m), this plant makes an outstanding contribution to the shrub border; it is also a good choice for a hedging plant.

▼ **Fall sunshine** From late summer onward, pride of place in the herbaceous border goes to the Michaelmas daisies *(Aster novi-belgii)*, whose splendid daisy flowers come in every shade of blue, pink, and purple. They are frequently partnered by perennial sunflowers *(Helianthus decapetalus)*, whose golden blooms glow in the autumn sunshine.

▶ **September color** Few shrubs flower in the fall garden and even fewer in the shade of purple-blue. *Hydrangea aspera aspera* is one exception; its large, flat lacy caps gleam against its velvety leaves when it is given the lightly shaded position it prefers. The purple theme is picked up and repeated here in the hydrangea's close companions, a dwarf sand cherry *(Prunus × cistena)* on one side and the purple-pink of *Anemone x hybrida* 'Mont Rose' on the other. Bright gold is supplied by the sprawling St.-John's-wort *(Hypericum* 'Hidcote') at the foot of the taller plants.

◀ **Winter miniatures** As early as January, the slender buds of *Crocus tomasinianus* push through the ground and at the merest kiss of sun open their pale lilac goblets to show off the golden stamens inside. They naturalize easily among other late-winter bulbs, such as golden aconites *(Eranthis hyemalis)* and hardy cyclamens like *Cyclamen hederifolium,* whose fall flowers have here given way to a carpet of handsome marbled leaves.

▶ **Shady rock gardens** A rock garden facing north or east is the favored site for many spring-flowering alpines — notably the anemonelike *Hepatica nobilis,* whose lavender-blue flowers seem flecked with gold dust. Primula hybrids *(P. x pubescens)* revel in similar conditions, their dense heads of mauve and deeper purple beautifully contrasting with the silver marbled leaves of *Cyclamen hederifolium.*

◀ **Spring bedding** The hardy hybrids of *Hyacinthus orientalis* include white and yellow, pink and red, and blue and purple named varieties. The deep purple-blue 'Ostara' creates a stunning carpet in late spring, embroidered here and there with the red splashes of a tiny bedding daisy *(Bellis perennis).*

BLUE AND PURPLE FLOWERS			
NAME	**DESCRIPTION AND SITE**	**HEIGHT**	**SEASON**
Buddleia alternifolia, B.davidii cvs.	Deciduous, arching habit; well-drained soil; sun	5-20 ft (1.5-6 m)	Early summer–fall
Callicarpa dichotoma	Deciduous, fall fruit; rich soil; sun or shade	4 ft (1.2 m)	Summer
Calluna vulgaris cvs.	Evergreen; well-drained acid soil; sun	1-3 ft (30-90 cm)	Summer–fall
Caryopteris x clandonensis	Deciduous, gray-green foliage; any soil; sun	4 ft (1.2 m)	Late summer
Ceanothus spp. and cvs.	Deciduous and evergreen; any soil; sun; shelter	6-20 ft (1.8-6 m)	Spring–fall
Ceratostigma willmottianum	Deciduous, half-hardy; loamy soil; sun; shelter	3 ft (90 cm)	Summer–fall
Clematis alpina, C. macropetala	Deciduous climbers; well-drained neutral soil; sun, roots in shade	6-12 ft (1.8-3.6 m)	Late spring–early summer
Corynabutilon vitifolium	Near-hardy; well-drained soil; sun; shelter	12 ft (3.6 m)	Summer
Daphne odora	Evergreen, glossy foliage; moist, well-drained soil; partial shade	4 ft (1.2 m)	Winter–spring
Fuchsia hybrids	Deciduous; moist loamy soil, sun or light shade	to 4 ft (1.2 m)	Summer–fall
Hebe spp. and cvs.	Near-hardy evergreen; moist, well-drained soil; sun	½-6 ft (15-180 cm)	Late spring–fall
Hibiscus syriacus 'Blue Bird'	Deciduous, upright; well-drained soil; sun	6-8 ft (1.8-2.4 m)	Summer–fall
Hydrangea macrophylla 'Blue Billow'	Deciduous, rounded habit; moist loamy soil; light shade; shelter	3-5 ft (90-150 cm)	Late summer
Lavandula spp. and cvs.	Evergreen; well-drained soil; sun	1-4 ft (30-120 cm)	Summer
Lespedeza thunbergii	Deciduous, arching; well-drained soil; full sun	4-6 ft (1.2-1.8 m)	Late summer
Passiflora caerulea	Semihardy evergreen climber; well-drained soil; sun; shelter	20 ft (6 m)	Summer–early fall
Perovskia atriplicifolia	Deciduous, excellent for coastal regions; well-drained soil; sun	3-5 ft (90-150 cm)	Summer–fall
Rhododendron 'Gable Hybrids'	Evergreen, leathery leaves; moist acid soil; light shade	2-4 ft (60-120 cm)	Spring
Robinia hispida	Deciduous; any soil; sun	6-10 ft (1.8-3 m)	Late spring
Rosmarinus officinalis	Evergreen, aromatic foliage; well-drained soil; sun	3-4 ft (90-120 cm)	Summer
Syringa vulgaris hybrids	Deciduous, fragrant; well-drained neutral soil; sun	8-12 ft (2.4-3.6 m)	Early summer
Vinca major, V. minor	Evergreen ground cover; any soil; shade	2-12 in (5-30 cm)	Spring–fall
Vitex agnus-castus	Deciduous; well-drained soil; sun	8-10 ft (2.4-3 m)	Late summer–fall
Wisteria sinensis	Deciduous vigorous climber; loamy soil; sun	25 ft (7.5 m)	Early summer
Ageratum houstonianum cvs.	Half-hardy, compact; moist soil; sun or light shade	5-12 in (12-30 cm)	Spring–fall
Anagallis arvensis caerulca	Hardy edging plant; any soil; sun	1-2 in (2.5-5 cm)	Summer–fall
Anchusa capensis	Hardy biennial, compact habit; moist soil; sun	9-18 in (23-45 cm)	Summer–fall
Callistephus chinensis hybrids	Half-hardy; well-drained soil; sun	½-3 ft (15-90 cm)	Summer
Campanula medium	Biennial, self-seeds; any soil; sun or light shade	1-3 ft (30-90 cm)	Late spring–summer
Centaurea cyanus cvs.	Hardy, easy, good for cutting; any soil; sun	1-3 ft (30-90 cm)	Summer–fall
Cobaea scandens	Half-hardy climber; well-drained soil; sun; shelter	10-20 ft (3-6 m)	Summer–fall
Felicia amelloides	Half-hardy, gray-green leaves; well-drained soil; sun	½-1½ ft (15-45 cm)	Summer
Heliotropium hybrids	Half-hardy, deeply fragrant; fertile soil; sun	1½-2 ft (45-60 cm)	Summer
Ipomoea purpurea	Half-hardy vigorous climber; light soil; sun; shelter	8-10 ft (2.4-3 m)	Summer–fall
Ipomoea tricolor	Half-hardy, bushy; good soil; sun; shelter	9-12 in (23-30 cm)	Summer-fall
Lobelia erinus cvs.	Half-hardy, compact or trailers; moist soil; sun	4-9 in (10-23 cm)	Late spring–fall
Lupinus nanus 'Pixie Delight'	Hardy, mixed strain; well-drained soil; sun or shade	1½ ft (45 cm)	Summer–fall
Nemophila menziesii	Hardy, compact, suitable for edging; moist soil; sun or light shade	6-9 in (15-23 cm)	Summer
Nierembergia repens	Half-hardy, attractive foliage; moist soil; sun	6-8 in (15-20 cm)	Summer–fall
Nigella damascena	Hardy, feathery foliage; any soil; sun	2 ft (60 cm)	Summer–fall
Salvia patens	Half-hardy, upright, branching; any soil; sun	2 ft (60 cm)	Late summer–fall

SHRUBS

ANNUALS AND BIENNIALS

PERENNIALS, BULBS, CORMS, AND TUBERS

NAME	DESCRIPTION AND SITE	HEIGHT	SEASON
Aconitum carmichaelii, A. napellus	Tough, branching; moist soil; light shade	3-6 ft (90-180 cm)	Summer–fall
Allium caeruleum, A. giganteum	Bulbous, attractive seed heads; well-drained soil; sun	2-5 ft (60-150 cm)	Early summer
Anchusa azurea	Branching, self-seeds; moist, well-drained soil; sun	3-5 ft (90-150 cm)	Summer
Anemone blanda, A. coronaria cvs.	Tuberous, ideal for naturalizing; well-drained soil; sun or light shade	½-1 ft (15-30 cm)	Early spring
Anemone pulsatilla	Downy buds, fernlike leaves, silky seed heads; well-drained soil; sun	8-12 in (20-30 cm)	Spring
Aquilegia flabellata, A. x hybrida cvs.	Rock and border plants; well-drained soil, sun or shade	1-2 ft (30-60 cm)	Late spring–summer
Aster x frikartii cvs.	Loose, bushy mounds; moist, well-drained soil; sun	2-3 ft (60-90 cm)	Early spring–fall
Brunnera macrophylla	Ground-cover plant; moist soil; light shade	12-15 in (30-38 cm)	Late spring–summer
Camassia cusickii, C. quamash	Bulbous; waterside or border plants; rich, moist soil; sun or light shade	2-3 ft (60-90 cm)	Early summer
Catananche caerulea	Suitable for drying; light soil; sun	1½-2½ ft (45-75 cm)	Summer
Centaurea montana	Clump forming, hairy leaves; well-drained soil; sun	2 ft (60 cm)	Late spring–summer
Chionodoxa spp.	Bulbous, spreads readily; well-drained soil; sun	4-8 in (10-20 cm)	Early spring
Clematis heracleifolia, C. integrifolia	Border plants, fluffy seed heads; neutral soil; sun or light shade	2-6 ft (60-180 cm)	Late summer
Colchicum 'Lilac Wonder'	Suitable for naturalizing; well-drained soil; sun or light shade	6-8 in (15-20 cm)	Fall
Cynoglossum nervosum	Hairy foliage; rich, moist soil; sun or light shade	1½-2 ft (45-60 cm)	Spring
Echinops spp.	Spiny leaves, good for drying; well-drained soil; drought-tolerant, sun	3-5 ft (90-150 cm)	Summer
Erigeron x hybridus cvs.	Clump forming, reliable; well-drained soil; sun	1-2½ ft (30-75 cm)	Summer
Eryngium spp.	Spiny leaves, prickly silver bracts; any soil; sun	1-3 ft (30-90 cm)	Summer
Fritillaria meleagris	Bulbous, good for naturalizing; well-drained soil; sun	10-12 in (25-30 cm)	Late spring
Galega officinalis	Bushy, wide-spreading; well-drained soil, sun or light shade	3-5 ft (90-150 cm)	Summer
Gentiana spp.	Herbaceous and evergreen rock and border plants; well-drained rich soil; sun or light shade	1-3 ft (30-90 cm)	Summer–fall
Geranium pratense cvs.	Border and edging plants; moist soil, sun	2-3 ft (60-90 cm)	Late spring
Iris spp. and cvs.	Bulbous and rhizomatous; well-drained soil; sun	½-3 ft (15-90 cm)	Spring–summer
Liatris spicata cvs.	Straight, strong stems; well-drained soil; sun	2-4 ft (6-120 cm)	Summer
Limonium latifolium	Clump forming; well-drained slightly acid soil; sun	2 ft (60 cm)	Summer
Linaria purpurea	Tall spikes, narrow leaves; any soil; sun	3 ft (90 cm)	Summer–fall
Linum narbonense	Free-flowering, narrow foliage; well-drained soil; sun	2 ft (60 cm)	Summer
Lobelia siphilitica	Tall flower spikes; rich, moist soil; light shade	3 ft (90 cm)	Late summer–fall
Meconopsis betonicifolia	Monocarpic; rich, moist soil; semishade; shelter	3-5 ft (90-150 cm)	Summer
Mertensia virginica	Easy-growing, blue-green foliage; rich, moist acid soil; shade	1-2 ft (30-60 cm)	Late spring
Muscari armeniacum, M. tubergenianum	Bulbous, strap-shaped leaves; any soil; sun or shade	8-10 in (20-25 cm)	Spring
Myosotis spp.	Prostrate or upright; moist soil; sun or light shade	6-8 in (15-20 cm)	Spring
Omphalodes cappadocica, O. verna	Carpeting plants; rich, moist soil; light shade	4-9 in (10-23 cm)	Spring
Polemonium caeruleum	Ferny foliage; any soil; sun or light shade	2 ft (60 cm)	Late spring–summer
Puschkinia scilloides	Bulbous, strap-shaped leaves; rich soil; sun	4-6 in (10-15 cm)	Spring
Salvia x superba cvs.	Bushy and branching, aromatic leaves; well-drained soil; sun	1½-3 ft (45-90 cm)	Summer
Sisyrinchium angustifolium, S. douglasii	Elegant narrow foliage; moist, well-drained soil; sun	10-12 in (25-30 cm)	Early spring–summer
Stokesia laevis	Easy, long-flowering; well-drained soil; sun or light shade	1-1½ ft (30-45 cm)	Summer–fall
Thalictrum delavayi	Handsome foliage, fluffy flower clusters; any moist soil; sun or light shade	2-4 ft (60-120 cm)	Spring–late summer
Tradescantia x andersoniana	Strap-shaped leaves, three-petaled flowers; well-drained soil; sun or light shade	1½-3 ft (45-90 cm)	Summer–fall
Veronica spp. and cvs.	Upright or mat forming, attractive foliage; well-drained soil; sun	3-48 in (7.5-120 cm)	Spring–summer

A riot of color

The resourceful gardener selects from the array of colors found in nature. Each plant offers a unique hue, and often a single species displays a parade of exciting colors through the seasons. But the experienced gardener knows, too, that colors give personality to flowers — and matching these personalities contributes to the success of a landscaping design. The gardener's task, then, is to find order hidden within nature's chaotic riches.

Often, for instance, annual flowers are considered too brash — their colors are deemed too bright and obvious. But annuals are perfect in a garden that is lit by the incandescent southern sun. Similarly, old-fashioned flowers and garden favorites of years past may offer hues no better than those of their modern counterparts. Yet a tangle of hollyhocks and old shrub roses creates a romantic atmosphere, offering a sense of nostalgia as well as pleasing color.

Fruits and berries usually play a supporting role in the color compositions of summer. However, they can become a truly dramatic centerpiece in the autumn garden, when their promise of fertility is an essential antidote as the foliage is dropping from trees and shrubs.

In our country's arid regions, succulents are not only practical plants for the dry spots in any garden, but essential suppliers of exotic, vibrant color as well. These drought-hardy sources of vivid flowers and foliage combine rugged self-sufficiency with flamboyant diversity.

Summer pathways A walkway winds past a border that bursts with color and variegated foliage.

MASSES OF SUMMER COLOR

**The hot months of summer bring
forth an explosion of color with old-fashioned
favorites and careful combinations.**

To compete with summer's azure skies, a garden must display equally bold effects — especially in the South, where the intense summer sunshine can wash out the more subtle tones of certain flowers. But one or two strong colors aren't enough. This is the season when you need to plant masses of flowers, especially those that have a bold, striking appearance. Annuals such as marigolds, salvias, and pelargoniums (commonly known as geraniums) are perfect choices for the summer garden. Their bright flowers, which can seem almost gaudy in another setting, provide a perfect complement for the summer heat and strong light.

The secret of mixing annuals into an eye-pleasing grouping is to temper the most vibrantly hued flowers, such as French marigolds *(Tagetes patula)*. You can do this by interplanting them with the cooler tones of flowers such as blue salvia. But be careful not to juxtapose clashing colors or textures in your groupings. Instead, interpose foliage plants such as the castor bean *(Ricinus communis)* or Dusty miller *(Senecio cineraria)* to act as color buffers. Above all, remember to plant generously — there shouldn't be an inch of earth visible when the plants are in bloom.

For a more sophisticated look than an annual bed can usually provide, try borrowing an idea from a traditional country garden. Fill the borders with old-fashioned favorites that provide color and perfume yet are sturdy and relatively carefree. If mingled in an unruly tangle, these flowers create an exuberant effect. Set the tallest plants — the delphiniums and shrub roses — to the rear. Save the hollyhocks to frame a doorway, and fill the foreground with pinks, catmint, and poppies. Don't overdesign; there is charm in a cluttered, unstudied look.

▼ **Floral carpet** Marigolds, begonias, geraniums, and salvias flower throughout the summer, delighting the eye with a profusion of vivid colors.

▲ **Summer riot** A brick path winds past an idyllic summer
scene towards a deliciously scented honeysuckle (*Lonicera
periclymenum* 'Beligca') and a clematis. Scarlet blooms
of the tall *Papaver orientale* glow above white *Hesperis
matronalis* 'Alba,' clumps of deep blue *Iris sibirica* and,
at the front, sprawling rose-pink *Centaurea dealbata*.

▶ **Filling the gaps** Annual love-in-a-mist (*Nigella damascena*)
is ideal for completing odd spaces in a border. Its pastel-blue
flowers, set among pale green, feathery foliage, bloom for
many sunny weeks and are followed by handsome brown seed
capsules. Poppies (*Papaver rhoes* 'Ladybird') make fiercely
crimson highlights amidst the blue cloud.

▼ **Tall and stately** A narrow bed seems wider with a clever backdrop of old-fashioned hollyhocks *(Alcea)*. The sturdy bloom-studded stems tower above a veil of seeding branches from the giant sea kale *(Crambe cordifolio)* and a front edging of white musk mallows *(Malva moschata* 'Alba').

◀ **Crimson symphony**
Carmine spikes of Russell lupines almost match a porcelain-pink climbing rose while contrasting in color and form with the lushly rounded blooms of double-flowered peonies. Crimson sweet Williams *(Dianthus barbatus)* add yet another shade of red in the foreground, relieved by a group of deep blue *Campanula glomerata.*

▼ **Profusion in the border**
Perfect, lilac-pink puffs of the 4-ft (1.2-m) tall *Allium giganteum* jostle for attention with white Shasta daisies *(Chrysanthemum maximum)* and double-flowered salmon-orange poppies *(Papaver orientale)*, which nestle close to the yellow and orange pea flowers of shrubby *Anthyllis hermanniae.* The yellow buttercups in the front are almost lost to the eye in this busy, early-summer scene.

GARDEN FRUITS

Berries and other fruits bring spots of color that liven up a landscape and extend its year-round appeal.

Many gardeners treat the berries that appear in their gardens as a welcome accident. But this extra harvest of color can be deliberately incorporated into a garden design. Berries and other fruits provide dramatic garden effects, adding sparkle to a mass of cool foliage in summertime or enlivening a winter scene.

On shrubs, trees, and vines throughout the garden you will find fruits of nearly every possible color. In addition to the scarlet of holly berries there is the fine china blue of the porcelain vine *(Ampelopsis brevipedunculata),* the white buttons of the snowberry *(Symphoricarpos albus),* the orange of pyracanthas, the brilliant yellow of crabapple 'Winter Gold,' and the lime green of the bower actinidia *(Actinidia arguta).*

Some plants bear their fruit so heavily that the bunches become a focal point in the garden. Few flowers can compete with the beautyberry bush *(Callicarpa dichtoma)* when summer wraps clusters of violet berries around its twigs like beads on a string. In regions such as the Southwest, where fall doesn't bring a foliar display, a cotoneaster's red fruits may be the only seasonal display in a garden bed. But typically berries serve more to flavor the dominant hues of surrounding flowers and leaves with a touch of vivid contrast.

Many berries also serve to attract another type of color, one no garden should be without — the colorful plumage of songbirds. Although the plump orange fruits that cling to the persimmon's branches long after the leaves have fallen make a rich spectacle by themselves, the sapphire flash of a blue jay coming for its favorite food completes the picture.

▲ **Winter decoration** The partnership of foliage, flowers, and fruit make holly one of the special ornaments of the garden. The white spring flowers and silver-edged leaves of this English holly *(Ilex aquifolium)* create a subtle harmony. In winter, its bright red berries liven up a winter scene.

▼ **Blazing color.** The aptly named "firethorn" *(Pyracantha coccinea)* explodes into a cloud of fiery orange-red berries in late summer. In this casual scene it poses a cheerful contrast to the yellow fall foliage of a grape vine.

▲ **Amber ornaments** The oriental persimmon *(Diospyros kaki)* retains its golden fruits after its leaves have fallen. A hardier native American relative, *Disopyros virginiana*, bears similar, though smaller, fruits as far north as central New England.

▲ **Showy red** It's easy to overlook the tiny white flowers of the red clusterberry *(Cotoneaster lacteus)*, because these little applelike fruits are the real show. From zone 6 southward, this shrub can form a hedge 12 ft (3.6m) tall. Hardier species of cotoneasters furnish similar displays even in the coldest regions.

▶ **Clusters of violet**
Edible and ornamental, the blueberry's elegant fruits make this shrub an asset anywhere in the landscape. Tolerant of some shade, blueberries will thrive only in acid soil. To ensure a bountiful yield of brilliant blue berries, plant at least two varieties.

◀ **Purple haze** A northern representative of a southern family, the beautyberry *(Callicarpa dichotoma)* lends a tropical flair to a landscape with its garlands of violet berries. This shrub grows 2-4 ft (60-120 cm) tall and makes an excellent background for a perennial border filled with the purple of fall asters.

SUCCULENTS

Increasingly popular in areas where water must be conserved, these drought-resistant plants offer a distinctive source of garden color.

As water becomes a scarce and expensive resource in many parts of North America, gardeners are looking for less thirsty alternatives to conventional garden plants. Succulents — plants that store moisture in their fleshy stems and leaves — offer a way for gardeners to reduce irrigation needs. But if succulents are practical, they are also beautiful; and they can present a unique source of garden color.

Cacti are the best-known succulents, but the group includes many other varities of plants, such as aloes (which are related to the lily) and agaves (relatives of the amaryllis). Though most of these plants prefer a warm, dry climate, some succulents will flourish in any part of the country. Given a fast-draining, sunny location, most thrive in the humidity of the Southeast. And several types, notably sempervivums and sedums, are winter hardy well into the north.

Succulents contribute color in two ways. Many bear flowers that combine exceptional delicacy of form with spectacular size and flamboyant hues. Prickly pears *(Opuntia spp.)*, which grow wild as far north as Massachusetts, reward the gardener with wheel-shaped blossoms of golden yellow or intense rose-pink that are 2 in (5 cm) or more across. The hues that suffuse the pads, stems, and fleshy leaves of succulents also provide interest. *Sedum rubrotinctum*, for example, edges its green foliage with red, while other species of this genus sport crimson or purple.

Because succulents are such a diverse group, they can substitute for most types of landscape plants. A stately saguaro provides a fine vertical accent and a moisture-saving substitute for a flowering tree, while hardy ice plants *(Delosperma* spp.) spread carpets of green, yellow, and purple flowers as ground cover. An imaginative design might combine the delicate, flowerlike rosettes of echeverias and boldly variegated century plants *(Agave americana marginata)* with dryland perennials such as achilleas to make a striking and drought-proof border.

▼ **Splendor year round** A well-balanced assortment of succulents fill this front yard with dramatic colors — and give it a lush look throughout the year with almost no irrigation.

▲ **Brilliant displays** Almost 2 in (5 cm) across, the incandescent flowers of these cob cacti *(Lobivia arachnacantha)* are nearly as large as the plants themselves. Outstanding for their flowers' brilliant colors, cacti are among the garden's most generous bloomers.

▶ **Dramatic contrast** The cool blue-green of this prickly pear's stout pads creates a theatrical setting for its delicate rosy blossoms. In many species, the green, yellow, red, or purple fruits of this perennial succulent are edible.

▼ **Durable delicacy** Few traditional flowers can withstand as much sun and drought as this Coral Aloe *(Aloe striata).* This graceful candelabra bears its reddish-orange flowers in spring. In full sun, its leaves become suffused with red streaks.

▲ **Golden armor** Spines are meant to ward off predators — but they can serve as source of color as well. The gilded armament of the golden barrel cactus *(Echinocactus grusonii)* gives this plant both its name and its visual appeal.

▼ **Low-care color** Cacti and yellow-flowered euphorbias blend easily with dryland flowers and shrubs in this southwestern yard, creating a garden that looks natural and requires almost no upkeep.

▲ **Blush of rose** Commonly called "hens and chicks" because of the way each mature rosette is surrounded by a flock of offspring, *sempervirums* are among the most hardy of succulents. They can thrive as far north as zone 3.

◄ **Vinelike habits** Its sprawling stems — 10 ft (3 m) long or more — make this climbing aloe (Aloe ciliaris) a water-thrifty substitute for conventional flowering vines. Other aloes, which may grow up to 60 ft (18 m) tall, can easily stand in for a flowering tree, while still others can fill a shrub's niche.

▼ **Carpets of color** Red-tipped leaves make Sedum rubrotinctum the centerpiece of this garden detail. Other sedums offer purple, blue, and yellow foliages as well as sheets of starry rose, white, or yellow flowers. These plants create unmatched ground covers for dry, rocky sites, and many are hardy through New England and onto the prairies.

INDEX

ACKNOWLEDGMENTS

Photo credits
Richard Balfour 123; Gillian Beckett 24(br); Biofotos/Heather Angel 21, 82, 101(b); Linda Burgess 110(b), 136; Ed Buziak 44 – 45; back cover; Eric Crichton 4 – 5, 6, 7, 8, 12(br), 17, 23(b), 24(t), 36(tr), 40, 46(tl), 46 – 47(b), 47(b), 48(t,l,b), 55 (tl,r), 61, 65, 70(tl), 72(t), 73(b), 74(b), 78, 81(tr,b), 93, 98(b), 102(br,bl), 112(b), 114(b), 122(l), 124(t,b), 126 (tl), 128(b), 130(t), 137(b), 140(t,b), 142(tl), 144(t), 145, 148(tr), 150(t), 158(b), 162, 164 – 165(b), (Eaglemoss) 28(b), 30(t), 32(b), 114(t); Arnaud Descat 89, 112(t), 125, 155(t); Derek Fell 134, 145, 167(b), 170(tl), 171(tl,b); Philippe Ferret 13(b), 68(b), 84, 85, 119, 156(b); Garden Picture Library (Brian Carter) 36(b), 37(b), 38(b), 46 – 47(tr), 52, 66(t), 96(t), 102(tr), 116, 142(tr), 147(tl), 150, 151, (John Glover) 45(tr), 47(tr), (Marijke Heuff) 142(b), (Anne Kelley) 166(t), (Anthony Paul) 152, (Jerry Pavia) 144(b), (Joanne Pavia) 96(b), 111, (Perdereau/Thomas) 9, 11(b), 70(bl), 71(b), 84(t), 155(b), 171(b), (David Russell) 23(t), (R. Sutherland) 54(tl), 56(b), 148(b),

(Brigitte Thomas) 64(b), 71(b), 148(b), (Didier Willery) 36(tl), (Steven Wooster) 113; John Glover 12(t), 19(bl,br), 20(b), 83, 101(t), 157(b); Derek Gould 34(b); Pamela Harper 137(b); Jerry Harpur 79, 81(tl), 109(t) 122(r), 166(b), (Abbots Ripton Hall, Cambs) 74(tr), (Chris Grey Wilson) 164 – 165(t), (Simon Hornby) 109(b), (Tintinhull House) 121, (John Vellum) 27; Grant Heilman (John Colwell) 168(tr), (Jane Grushow) 168(bl); Marijke Heuff 57, 58; Neil Holmes 24(bl), 70 – 71; Saxon Holt 168(tl), 169, 170(b), 172(b); Insight/Linda Burgess 72(b), 100(t); Lamontagne 90, 91, 107, 108, 117, 118, 150(b); Andrew Lawson 16(t), 53, 54(tr), 56(t), 94, 95(t), 98 – 99; S & O Mathews 14 – 15, 16(b), 86(t), 126(b), 134, 146(b); Tania Midgley 39, 40 – 41, 41(tr), 54(b), 99(b); Natural Image (Bob Gibbons) 48(tr), 66(b), 67, (Liz Gibbons) 146(t); Philippe Perdereau 26, 31, 32 – 33, 42, 55(b), 59, 92(r), 110(t), 115, 120(l), 137(t), 138(b), (Brigitte Thomas) 2 – 3, 10, 15(b), 69, 95(b), 97; Clay Perry 138(t); Photo Nats (Tovah Martin) 19(br); (Robert E. Lyons) 172(t), Peter Margosian 170(tr); Photos Horticultural 18(t), 22, 35, 38(t), 44(t), 71(tr), 86(bl), 87, 88, 127(b);

Positive Images (Jerry Howard) 167(tr), 171(tr); Harry Smith Collection 37(t), 43, 86(tl), 128(tr) 129(t,b), 156(t); Jean-Pierre Soulier 60, 62, 92(l), 126(tr), 153, 154(b); EWA 106, 120(r), (Karl Dietrich Bukler) 141, (Jerry Harpur) front cover, 64(t), 73(t), 98(tl), 148(tl).

Illustrations
Ali Christie 1; Reader's Digest 20(t), 28(t), 29(tr,br), 30(b), 62, 66, 68, 84, 85, 94, 99, 100, 118, 121, 122, 135, 136(b), 138, (Dick Benson) 157, (Leonara Box) 19(t), 58, 60, 63, 80, 90, 108, 130(b), 138, (Patricia Calderhead) 82, 114, (Lynn Chadwick) 136(t), (Sara Fox Davies) 39, 41(tl), 59, 87, 89, (Brian Delf) 33(b), (Colin Emberson) 96, 102(tl), (Shirley Fells) 18(b), 88, 127, (Delyth Jones) 33(t), 44(b), 120, 165, (Nikki Kemball) 95, 146, (Josephine Martin) 107, 117, (Helen Senior) 91, (Sally Smith) 128, (Sue Stitt) 13(t), 65, 92, 115, 143, (Gill Tomblin) 12(bl), 14(b), 34(t), 42, 119, 158, (Barbara Walker) 11(t), 15(t), 109, 154(tr), (Ann Winterbotham) 141, 168.

Index compiled by Kate Chapman.